SPECTRUM®

Vocabulary

Grade 4

SPECTRUM®

Greensboro, NC

Spectrum®
An imprint of Carson-Dellosa Publishing LLC
P.O. Box 35665
Greensboro, NC 27425 USA

Printed in the USA • All rights reserved.   ISBN 978-0-7696-8084-2

07-028137784

Table of Contents

Skills Practice

Test-taking Practice

Name _____

Classifying means to put objects together in **groups**.
   Feet, **yards**, and **inches** are all **measurements**.
   Softball, **football**, and **soccer** are all **sports**.

Cross out the word in each group that does not belong. Then write a word from the word box that does belong.

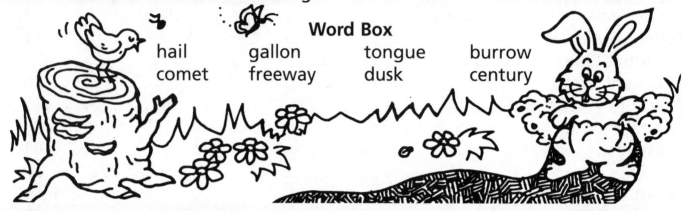

Word Box

hail	gallon	tongue	burrow
comet	freeway	dusk	century

1. sun planet stars moon violin meteor _____	2. eyes foot teeth nose ears cheeks _____	
3. teaspoon liter quart cup pint several _____	4. nest barn library cave hive den _____	
5. path highway trail street car road _____	6. lightning storm thunder mutter rain blizzard _____	
7. sunrise dinner morning noonday afternoon evening _____	8. paddle decade month year day hour _____	

Name _____

Cross out the word in each row that does not belong.

1. discus   football   basketball   gumball

2. boot   sandal   sock   clog

3. camera   watch   calendar   clock

4. hand   foot   head   hat

5. lemon   cherry   orange   grapefruit

6. bicycle   buggy   jeep   bed

7. glasses   window   windshield   toupee

8. surgeon   dentist   lawyer   veterinarian

9. backpack   book   bucket   purse

10. microwave   toaster   refrigerator   teakettle

Name _____

An analogy uses word relationships to compare one group to another group.

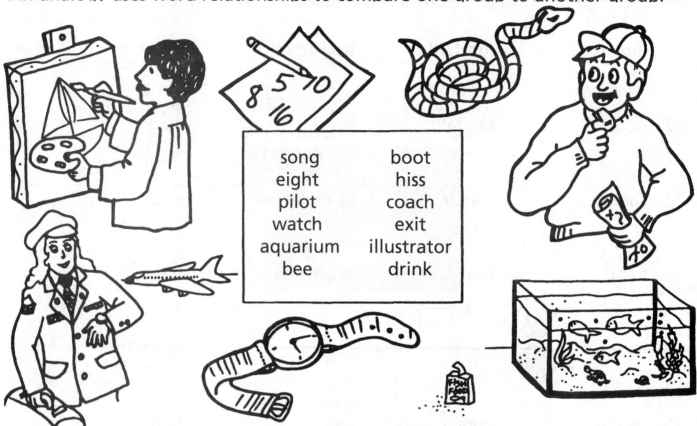

song	boot
eight	hiss
pilot	coach
watch	exit
aquarium	illustrator
bee	drink

Choose the word from the word box that completes each analogy.

1. Teacher is to student as _____coach_____ is to player.

2. Five is to ten as _____ is to sixteen.

3. Writer is to book as _____ is to picture.

4. Ring is to finger as _____ is to arm.

5. Driver is to bus as _____ is to airplane.

6. Meow is to cat as _____ is to snake.

7. Out is to in as _____ is to enter.

8. Cage is to parakeet as _____ is to fish.

9. Eat is to hungry as _____ is to thirsty.

10. Story is to read as _____ is to sing.

11. Bear is to den as _____ is to hive.

12. Glove is to hand as _____ is to foot.

Name _____

Write each word from the word box in the correct continent list.

penguin	blue whale	emu	fur seal
beaver	wolverine	giraffe	Canadian lynx
cheetah	moose	koala	orca
hyena	camel	kangaroo	dingo

Africa

_____   _____

_____   _____

Australia

_____   _____

_____   _____

North America

_____   _____

_____   _____

Antarctica

_____   _____

_____   _____

Cross out the word that does not belong. Then write a word from the word box that does belong.

| nightstand | cupboard | tulips | pen | tools | hat |

1. markers   cookie
    eraser   notebook
    book   glue
    _____

2. bed   blanket
    penguin   dresser
    comforter   pillow
    _____

3. table   chair
    refrigerator   car
    toaster   blender
    _____

4. sweater   pants
    skirt   raisin
    shoes   shirts
    _____

5. lawnmower   shovel
    garbage can   hose
    watering can   tomato
    _____

6. roses   daisies
    cucumbers   tomatoes
    rain   squash
    _____

Name _____

Write each word from the word box in the correct category to complete the list of foods.

Spices	Desserts	Drinks	Grains/Breads
_____	_____	_____	_____
_____	_____	_____	_____
_____	_____	_____	_____
_____	_____	_____	_____
_____	_____	_____	_____
_____	_____	_____	_____
_____	_____	_____	_____
_____	_____	_____	_____

apple dumpling	bagel	barley	cereal	cider	cinnamon	cloves
cobbler	cola	cracker	cumin	curry	eclair	eggnog
fudge	ginger	hot cocoa	juice	milk shake	milk	nutmeg
oatmeal	paprika	pasta	pepper	wassail	rice	sorbet
strudel	tortilla	truffle	pumpkin pie			

Name _____

Synonyms are words that mean the **same** thing.
    Big and **huge** are **synonyms**.
    Tiny and **small** are **synonyms**.

Circle the synonym for each word.

ugly	humbly	hasty	homely	hosiery
mean	vicious	vigorous	various	valiant
kind	generate	generous	genius	general
beautiful	eloquent	elevate	element	elegant

Write a paragraph using the four words you circled.

_____

_____

_____

_____

_____

_____

_____

_____

Name _____

Write a synonym for each word from the word box.

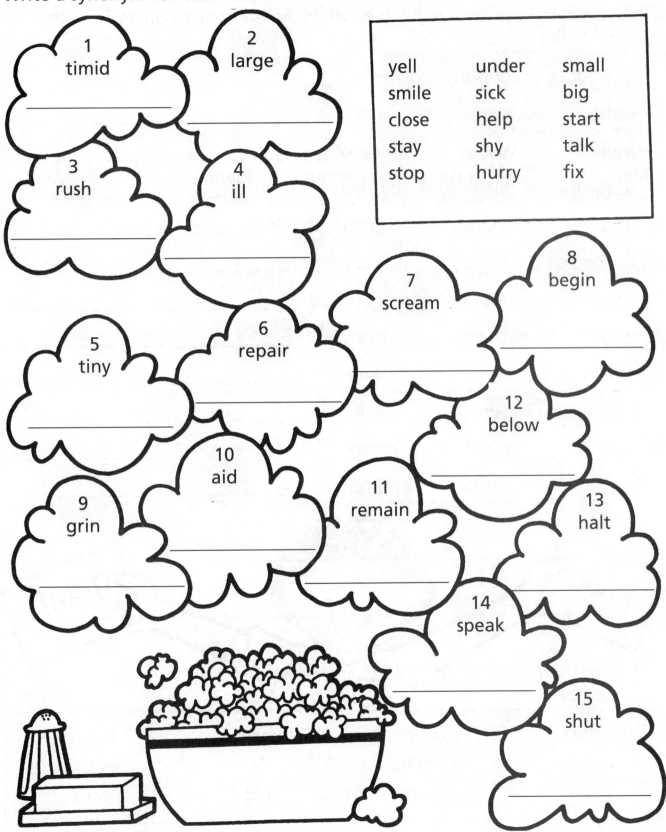

yell	under	small
smile	sick	big
close	help	start
stay	shy	talk
stop	hurry	fix

1. timid _____

2. large _____

3. rush _____

4. ill _____

5. tiny _____

6. repair _____

7. scream _____

8. begin _____

9. grin _____

10. aid _____

11. remain _____

12. below _____

13. halt _____

14. speak _____

15. shut _____

Name _____

Circle a synonym for the <u>underlined</u> word. Write another synonym from the word box on the line.

1. <u>intelligent</u>   bright   friendly   _____

2. <u>assist</u>   repair   aid   _____

3. <u>frigid</u>   chilly   weather   _____

4. <u>puzzled</u>   mean   baffled   _____

5. <u>bravery</u>   boldness   frighten   _____

6. <u>dangerous</u>   huge   hazardous   _____

7. <u>easy</u>   careful   uncomplicated   _____

8. <u>trade</u>   exchange   buy   _____

9. <u>repair</u>   sell   mend   _____

10. <u>happiness</u>   joy   smile   _____

11. <u>calm</u>   quiet   pretty   _____

12. <u>power</u>   loud   strength   _____

gladness	courage	simple	help
risky	confused	fix	swap
smart	force	cold	peace

Name _____

Antonyms are words that mean the **opposite**.
    Big and **small** are **antonyms**.
    Hot and **cold** are **antonyms**.

Look at the picture and read the sentence. Circle the word that does not make sense. Then write the word that would make the sentence true.

1. Pam is surprised because there is something in the box. _____ nothing everything		2. The plane will leave at one o'clock.  _____ runway arrive
3. Tim doesn't know that there is a bee on the front of his shirt. _____ sleeve back		4. When you set the table, place the fork on the right side of the plate.  _____ left same
5. Kim is sad because she found the missing bunny. _____ tired happy		6. He stayed in bed because he was well.  _____ sick young

Name _____

Write the antonym for each word.

innocent	present	interior	victory	doubt	rare
defense	increase	shallow	few	wild	plain
departure	minimum	excited	lazy	smooth	rude

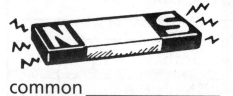  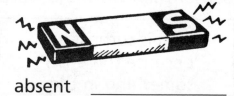

common _____ fancy _____ absent _____

deep _____ many _____ maximum _____

rough _____ polite _____ arrival _____

ambitious _____ decrease _____ offense _____

exterior _____ defeat _____ believe _____

calm _____ guilty _____ tame _____

Name _____

Circle the pair of antonyms in each box. Complete each sentence with one of the circled words.

| sweet | quiet | noisy | fast |

1. The blowing horns were _____.

2. It was _____ in the library.

| rough | empty | smooth | straight |

3. The cat's fur felt _____.

4. The sandpaper was _____.

| close | wrong | near | right |

5. Never drive the _____ way on a one-way street.

6. It was _____ in the library.

| bought | decorated | sent | sold |

7. I _____ my old bike when I outgrew it.

8. Mom _____ me a warmer jacket.

| laugh | sleepy | lose | find |

9. Did you _____ the key I lost?

10. In a strange place, it's easy to _____ your way.

| break | own | hurt | repair |

11. A flying ball might _____ a window.

12. He needed tools to _____ the car.

Name _____

Read each sentence. Circle the word that does not make sense in the sentence. Then rewrite the sentence using the antonym for the circled word.

huge	dangerous	exit	drenched
future	better	raw	frown

1. The elephant was (tiny)

   The elephant was huge.
   _____

2. It is safe to touch electric wires.

   _____

3. After the rain the ground was dry.

   _____

4. A cooked carrot is hard and crunchy.

   _____

5. This medicine should make you feel worse.

   _____

6. The overdue book notice made me smile.

   _____

7. In the past I plan to go to college.

   _____

8. Go out through the entrance.

   _____

Name _____

Write a synonym and antonym for each word below.

	Synonym	Antonym
1. shut	_____	_____
2. heal	_____	_____
3. chilly	_____	_____
4. whole	_____	_____
5. steal	_____	_____
6. sent	_____	_____
7. bare	_____	_____
8. win	_____	_____
9. male	_____	_____
10. tall	_____	_____
11. gift	_____	_____
12. girl	_____	_____
13. glass	_____	_____
14. clip	_____	_____
15. lamp	_____	_____

Name _____

Homonyms are words that **sound the same** but **mean different things.**
They are sometimes **spelled differently**, too.
   Know and **no** are **homonyms.**
   Weigh and **way** are **homonyms.**

Use the picture clues to help you choose the correct word for each sentence.
Write the word on the line.

1. I got a letter in the
_____.

male   mail

2. The dog's _____
made muddy prints.

paws   pause

3. She was gone for an
_____.

hour   our

4. My favorite
_____ is a rose.

scents   cents

5. Buy now and save
ten _____.

scents   cents

6. We chopped
_____ for a fire.

would   wood

7. He hung the
_____ to dry.

close   clothes

8. We nailed the
_____ in place.

board   bored

9. I can _____
my name in cursive.

right   write

10. The _____
will be sunny.

weather   whether

11. Our team _____
the pennant.

won   one

12. I like to read
_____.

allowed   aloud

Name _____

Write a homonym, antonym, and synonym for each word below.

	Homonym	Synonym	Antonym
1. son			
2. heal			
3. chilly			
4. whole			
5. steal			
6. sent			
7. bare			
8. won			
9. male			
10. high			
11. sell			
12. fair			

Name _____

Write a homonym that fits both clues.

1. where we live / the soil

2. branch of a tree / arm or leg

Homonyms

nail	well
limb	earth
deck	saw
safe	bill
star	bat

3. not sick / deep hole with water

4. part of a bird's mouth / something you pay

5. part of a ship / group of cards

6. used to cut wood / had seen something

7. not risky / place to keep money

8. in the sky / a famous person

9. on your finger / hit with a hammer

10. for hitting a ball / lives in caves

Name _____

Write the missing word in each sentence.

| flee
flea | 1. My dog has a _____ on his tail.
2. Did the cats _____ when the dog barked? |

| beats
beets | 3. Mother _____ the eggs with the mixer.
4. Those _____ are from the garden. |

| right
write | 5. Please _____ me a letter soon.
6. I lost my _____ shoe! |

| scent
cent | 7. I like the _____ of the spices.
8. I have one _____ in my pocket. |

| won
one | 9. We _____ the game.
10. I have _____ dollar in the bank. |

| dew
due | 11. The book is _____ on Friday.
12. The grass is wet from _____ . |

| no
know | 13. Do you _____ her name?
14. There is _____ more candy. |

| creek
creak | 15. Frogs live in the _____ .
16. Does that door _____ when opened? |

Name _____

Read each pair of words in the word box. Read the clues and complete the puzzle using one of the words from each pair.

sale-sail	whole-hole	sent-cent	pair-pear	our-hour
dear-deer	plane-plain	no-know	write-right	ate-eight

Across

1. an animal with antlers

7. to travel across water

8. 60 minutes of time

9. the opposite of yes

10. a penny

Down

2. the number before nine

3. the opposite of wrong

4. a set of two

5. a flying machine

6. an opening

Name _____

Context Clues are clues you can find in a sentence to help you figure out **what a word means**.

Coins are made in factories called mints. The first mint in America was in Philadelphia. Plans for this mint were started by a resolution of Congress in April 2, 1792. The first coins struck, or made, in America were minted that same year. The first denomination was called a half-disme or half-dime. A year later, several other denominations of coins were struck, including the quarter-dollar, the disme or dime, the gold eagles (worth $10), and the copper cent.

It took a lot of work to mint coins. Before a coin could be manufactured, a die was made. In the late 1800s, these dies were cut by hand. First an exact drawing had to be made. Then the drawing was traced into wax. The wax was used as a pattern to form steel. Finally a die, or mold, was finished which could be used to strike coins. Since this work was done by hand, the coins had small differences each time a new die was made.

Today, coins are standardized. Although hundreds of dies are used each year to make a denomination of coin, each die is made from a master die. Machines and computers are also used in this process so that the minted coins look alike. The only differences are the dates and the location codes which show where each coin is made.

Read the passage about coins.

Choose the best meaning by placing an X in the correct blank.

1. What is the meaning of the word *mint* as used in this article?
   __a piece of candy   __a factory where coins are made   __a lot of money

2. What is the meaning of the word *strike* as used in this article?
   __to cross out   __to attack   __to make by stamping

3. What is the meaning of the word *die* as used in this article?
   __a mold   __to color with a stain or paint   __to stop living

4. What is the meaning of the word *standardized* as used in this article?
   __original   __the same every time   __a flag

5. What is the meaning of the word *denomination* as used in this article?
   __having the same size and value   __color   __sharing the same beliefs

Name _____

Use the context clues to help you choose the correct word to complete each sentence.

 **desert** — very dry land

 **dessert** — after-meal treat

1. Dad made us pudding for a special

_____.

2. We drove across miles of sandy

_____.

 **lose** — misplace

loose — not tight

3. My brother's sweater was too

_____.

4. The money is in my pocket so I won't

_____ it.

 **single** — only, one

signal — warning sign

6. The red light was a

5. The _____
letter in the mailbox was for me.

_____ to stop.

Name _____

Use the context clues to help you replace the underlined word with a synonym from the word box.

center	job
lay	strict
utmost	silliness

1.) "I am shocked to the core _____ of my being! What nonsense _____ is this when you choose to drape _____ your wet coat over our precious antique love seat? Be aware that stringent _____ attention to our museum's guidelines is of vital _____ importance if you wish to retain your post _____!"

crossed	studied
helpful	newsstand
asked	return

2.) We collected a newspaper at the kiosk _____ and traversed _____ the intersection to retire _____ to the hotel. In the lobby, we perused _____ the local page. We hoped to find a movie listing, but could not locate one, so we inquired _____ at the front desk. The clerk was most contributive _____.

Name _____

Choose a word from the word box to replace the **boldfaced** word in each sentence. Use a dictionary to help you with new words.

1. We took a **trek** up the mountainside.

   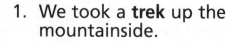

   _____

2. The meat was served on a large **platter**.

   _____

wrote	tray	real
trip	limp	wet
late	dry	force
winner	layer	reason

3. The crown had **genuine** diamonds.

   _____

4. She missed the bus so she was **tardy**.

   _____

5. Without an umbrella I got **drenched**.

   _____

6. The desert soil was **parched**.

   _____

7. He **scrawled** a message on paper.

   _____

8. A **film** of ice covered the street.

   _____

9. The hurt player had to **hobble** off the field.

   _____

10. The **impact** of the wind broke off the branch.

    _____

11. The blue ribbon went to the **victor**.

    _____

12. What **motive** did you have for doing this?

    _____

Name _____

Each sentence below contains a **heart** word or phrase. Choose a meaning from the word box. Write it on the line.

center	saddened	courage	loved one	friendly
honest	wanted	from memory	tender	

1.
We had a **heart-to heart** talk.

_____

2.
I had **soft-hearted** feelings for the puppy.

_____

3.
It's in the **heart** of the city.

_____

4.
I was **heartbroken** by the news.

_____

5.
I didn't have the **heart** to tell her.

_____

6.
I know that song **by heart**.

_____

7.
Grandma is a **sweetheart**.

_____

8.
He gave me a **hearty** welcome.

_____

9.
I **had my heart set on** the black kitten.

_____

Name _____

Write the correct word from each pair to complete the sentences.

series
serious

1. We had a _____ talk.

2. I've collected the whole _____.

united
untied

3. My shoe always comes _____.

4. We gave a _____ cheer for the team.

angel
angle

5. The ball bounced off at an _____.

6. The _____ costume was white.

weather
whether

7. I don't know _____ to buy it or not.

8. I hope the _____ will be nice.

intend
attend

9. I _____ to finish it soon.

0. I cannot _____ your party.

lose
loose

1. The knob on the radio is _____.

2. I hope you didn't _____ my phone number.

accept
except

3. I _____ your invitation to come.

4. Everyone was on time _____ me.

Name _____

Read the passage about television. Then answer the questions.

The name *television* comes from *tele-* meaning *far* in Greek, and *videre* meaning *to see* in Latin. Before 1950, the use of television was **rare**. Then, during a single **decade**, the ten-year period from 1950 to 1960, television became a part of almost every household in the United States. It **swiftly** became a **major** influence in people's lives. It changed the way they spent their time and let them see a whole new world right in their own homes.

Since the 1950s television has **evolved**, or grown and changed, to include uses in businesses, hospitals, schools, and law enforcement. As well as providing entertainment, television broadcasts business meetings and **monitors** hospital patients. It lets students study and observe world **events** as they happen, and even guards banks and prisons.

1. Which boldfaced word in the story means:
   a. a ten-year period?   _____
   b. quickly?   _____
   c. important?   _____
   d. grown and changed?   _____
   e. watches over?   _____
   f. happenings?   _____
   g. uncommon?   _____

2. Where did the name for television come from?

   _____

   _____

   _____

3. How did television influence people's lives after 1950?

   _____

   _____

4. What do you think is television's most important use and why?

   _____

   _____

Name _____

Concept words are words that have to do with a certain **topic** or **idea**.
   Multiply, fraction, and **division** are all **math** words.
   Mix, blend, spice, and **bake** are all **cooking** words.

Write each science from the word box in the correct category.

BETTER GRADES THRU SCIENCE!

fishing pole	hummingbird
stinkbug	poodle
telephone	aquarium
television	redwood tree
mushroom	roller skates
laser beam	space shuttle
meteor	tadpole
toucan	crocodile
warthog	walkie-talkie

Living   **Non-Living**

_____   _____

_____   _____

_____   _____

_____   _____

_____   _____

_____   _____

_____   _____

_____   _____

Name _____

Answer each clue with a **math** word from the word box and fill in the puzzle.

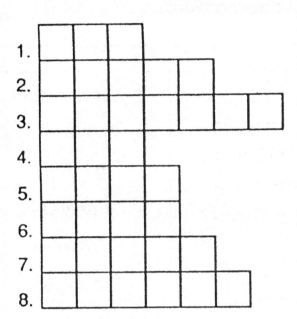

count

add

numbers

plus

minus

equals

even

odd

1. Begin at one and count to nineteen using _____ numbers.

2. If you begin at one, how high can you _____ ?

3. Fill in the chart with the _____ from 1 to 1000.

4. If you _____ six and two, you will have eight.

5. Two _____ six equals eight.

6. Begin at two and count to twenty using _____ numbers.

7. Three _____ one equals two.

8. Three minus one _____ two.

Name _____

Use the words in the word box to help you unscramble the animal names.

Across:

3. dhsifrows _____

5. slruaw _____

7. ttylfrueb _____

8. aob _____

13. dkarvraa _____

14. rwne _____

15. oosge _____

Down:

1. nswa _____

2. aierffg _____

4. tteearna _____

6. rrleiuqs _____

9. rssoatbla _____

11. worc _____

12. nnuigpe _____

penguin
swan
giraffe
anteater
crow
albatross
squirrel
wren
swordfish
walrus
goose
butterfly
boa
aardvark

Name _____

Use the clues on page 32 to complete the puzzle.

DON'T USE ANY CROSS WORDS!

Name _____

Read this story full of **science words**. Write each **boldfaced** word next to its meaning.

     Scientists are looking for new **sources**, or places, to get energy. They are finding new ways to make, or **produce**, the power we will need in the future.

     One kind of energy is **geothermal**. "Geo" means "earth" and "thermal" means "heat." Geothermal energy comes from heat that is already stored inside the earth.

     Another kind of energy is **solar**. "Sol" means "sun." The sunlight is changed into energy we can use.

1. _____ heat from the earth

2. _____ from the sun

3. _____ to make

4. _____ places to get something

These pictures show kinds of energy. Label them **geothermal** or **solar**.

5.

6.

_____   _____

Name _____

Sensory words are words that describe something you **smell, taste, touch, see** or **hear**. **Onomatopoeia** is a word that **describes a sound**.

Choose a word from the word box that describes each picture.

knock	quack	murmur	zoom
neigh	fizz	ding dong	slop

1. _____

2. _____

3. _____

4. _____

5. _____

6. _____

7. _____

8. _____

Name _____

Match the sense with the sensory word.

see	rough
touch	salty
hear	light
smell	whisper
taste	stinky

Write a sentence using each of the sensory words above.

1. _____

_____

2. _____

_____

3. _____

_____

4. _____

_____

5. _____

_____

Name _____

Rewrite each sentence with at least two sensory words from the word box or from your imagination.

red	shiny	mean
yellow	tiny	nasty
green	happy	excited
striped	silly	relieved
polka dotted	goofy	trusting
brown	ridiculous	confused
mangy	funny	
fluffy	hilarious	

1. I have a sweater.

_____

2. This is my brother.

_____

3. Where is my dog?

_____

4. Did you see that bird?

_____

5. I feel today.

_____

Name _____

Fill in each blank with a sensory word.

1. I've been sick for _____ days.

2. That cake is _____.

3. My friends are _____.

4. Can you come to my _____ party?

5. The band is _____.

Complete the poem using sensory words.

I see _____

_____

I hear _____

_____

I touch _____

_____

I smell _____

_____

I taste _____

_____

Name _____

Read each onomatopoeia word in the word box. Write a sentence explaining what made each noise.

1. drip _____

   _____

2. rustle _____

   _____

3. moan _____

   _____

4. crack _____

   _____

5. tap _____

   _____

6. thump _____

   _____

Name _____

A **plural** word is **more than one** of a person, place, or thing. Remember:
    Change **y** to **i** and add **es**.
    Words that end in **sh**, **ch**, **x**, or **z**, add **es**.
    Change **f** to **v** and add **es**.

Change each word to the plural form.

1. The _____ are hiding in the _____.
        squirrel   ditch

2. You will see _____ at many _____.
               seal   beach

3. Put the _____ in the _____.
            firefly   jar

4. How many _____ did you pick from the _____?
              berry   bush

5. Put the _____ in the _____.
            letter   mailbox

6. Put the _____ on the _____.
            brush   shelf

7. I bought two _____ for my _____.
                watch   friend

8. We saw ten _____ on three _____.
              bird   branch

9. I want two _____ for my _____.
              lollipop   sister

10. The _____ are taking their _____.
          baby   nap

Name _____

Make each word plural. Use the plural words to complete the sentences.

1. The two _____ of bread on the counter smelled delicious.

2. How many _____ do you think a chef would own?

3. _____ live in packs and look very much like dogs.

4. The _____ of the ship's passengers were in danger when the storm hit.

5. _____ of brilliant colors hung on the tree.

6. The _____ were filled with a variety of books.

7. All the oranges were cut into _____.

8. The store window was filled with _____ of all sizes and colors.

Name _____

Make the following words plural. Remember to add **es** to words that end in **s, x, z, ch, sh, ss,** and sometimes **o**.

1. ostrich   _____

2. buffalo   _____

3. camper   _____

4. balloon   _____

5. toothbrush _____

6. church   _____

7. caterpillar _____

8. lunch   _____

9. tomato   _____

10. paragraph _____

11. skateboard _____

12. volcano   _____

13. potato   _____

14. class   _____

15. sandbox   _____

16. notebook   _____

17. fossil   _____

BUFFALO? AIN'T THAT NEAR ROCHESTER?

Name _____

Change each word to the plural form. Write the word on the line.
Change **f** to **v** and add **es**.
Change **y** to **i** and add **es**.

1. The _____ are pretty colors.
   leaf

2. We picked _____ in the woods.
   berry

3. We saw a movie about _____ .
   wolf

4. The _____ are in the barn.
   calf

5. There are two _____ in the city.
   library

6. Dad built _____ in the garage.
   shelf

7. It costs a dollar to ride the _____ .
   pony

8. The story is about seven tiny _____ .
   elf

9. _____ are fun to watch at night.
   Firefly

10. Mother planted _____ in the yard.
    lily

11. The mother lion has three _____ .
    baby

12. The police caught the _____ .
    thief

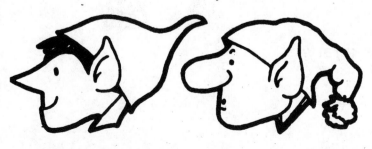

Name _____

A **suffix** is a part **added to the end** of a word. Suffixes change the meaning of words.

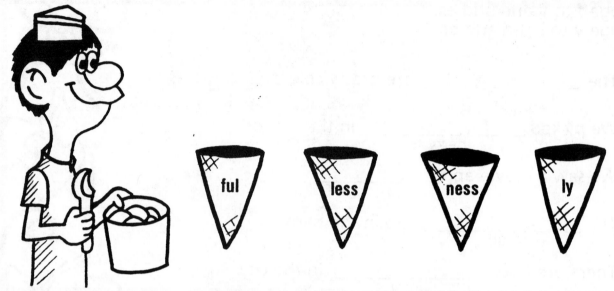

Add the suffix **ful, less, ness,** or **ly** to each word to complete the sentences.

1. Ann's little kitten is very play_____.

2. All of the trees are leaf_____ now.

3. I can hard_____ hear you.

4. We must work quick_____ to get done.

5. The red_____ of his nose made us laugh.

6. Mother cooked a bone_____ ham.

7. We are very thank_____ for this rain.

8. Their dogs bark night_____.

9. Please talk soft_____ in the library.

10. Thank you for being so help_____.

Name _____

Use the suffixes **er** and **est** to compare words.

1. A.    B.    C

Which one is fat? _____   fatter? _____   fattest? _____

2. A.   B.   C.

Which one is small? _____   smaller? _____   smallest? _____

3. Your turn to draw a picture
   A.   B.   C.

   thick   **thicker**   **thickest**

Add **er** and **est** to these words.

soft   _____   _____

cold   _____   _____

tall   _____   _____

slow   _____   _____

4. If you compare 2 things, use the ending _____.

5. If you compare 3 things or more, use _____.

Name _____

Complete the sentences by adding the suffix **er** and **est** to each word.

1. This is the _____ road of all.
2. My doll is the _____ of the three.
3. He is the _____ clown of all.
4. I couldn't be _____ !
5. Sue acts _____ than Jan.
6. This is the _____ day of the year.
7. Our dog is _____ than yours.
8. It is _____ for Bill than for me.
9. Saturday is Mom's _____ day.
10. Who is _____, you or Tim?
11. This nail is _____ than the other one.
12. John is the _____ boy in the world!

bumpy
pretty
funny
happy
silly
windy
lazy
easy
busy
sleepy
rusty
lucky

Name _____

Write the word that makes sense in the sentence. Circle each suffix.

rested	peaches
seedless	lumpy
making	spoonful
healthful	sweeten
farmer	boxes

1. Alice picked some ripe _____ for Grandmother.

2. That _____ grows strawberries, too.

3. These berries will _____ my cereal.

4. Dad is _____ a tasty banana bread.

5. Tracy likes _____ grapes the best.

6. An orange is a _____ dessert.

7. Put a _____ of blueberries in the batter.

8. Bill likes raisins; they make his oatmeal _____ .

9. I can help you put the apples in _____ .

10. After picking cherries, we _____ .

Name _____

Add the suffix **less, ful, er, ly** or **ness** to each word. Write it on the line.

1. care_____ 2. sing _____ 3. rapid_____

less

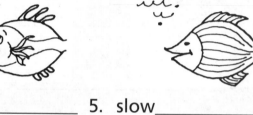 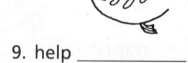

4. dark_____ 5. slow_____ 6. bank_____

ful

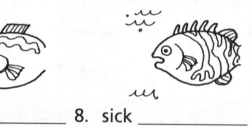 

7. play _____ 8. sick _____ 9. help _____

er

 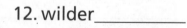

10. friend_____ 11. cup _____ 12. wilder_____

ly

 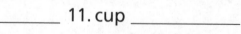 

ness

13. rude_____ 14. teach_____ 15. quiet _____

Name _____

Read the suffixes and their meanings in the word box.
Then write the word that correctly completes each
sentence.

able	—	like, capable of
en	—	to make
ful	—	full of
ist	—	one who
ize	—	to make

less	—	without, lack of
ly	—	in the manner of
ment	—	act or quality of
ness	—	state or quality of
ous	—	full of, having the quality of

1. There was much (excitement, excitable) at the art gallery. _____

2. A well-known (artful, artist) was going to put on a painting

   workshop. _____

3. Everyone was in (agreement, agreeable) that the workshop would

   be interesting. _____

4. People lined up (eagerly, eagerness) to enter the gallery. _____

5. As the people streamed into the gallery, they gazed in (wonderment, wonderful) at the

   beautiful sculptures near the doorway. _____

6. The people were (careful, careless) not to bump into the

   sculptures. _____

7. Some people stopped to admire a painting of a (glamorous, glamorize)

   movie star. _____

8. Soon the painter arrived and everyone clapped (loudly, loudness). _____

9. The painter smiled (politely, politeness) and set up his materials. _____

10. He began by showing how a person could (brighten, brightly) pictures using just the

    right colors. _____

11. He also showed how a quick (movable, movement) with the paintbrush could produce an

    interesting stroke. _____

12. When the workshop was over, everyone agreed it had been a (memorize, memorable)

    art lesson. _____

Name _____

A **prefix** is a part **added to the beginning** of a word. Prefixes change the meanings of words.

HI THERE! I'M PETE AND THIS IS MY SON, REPETE! SAY HELLO, REPETE!

HELLO, REPETE!

The prefix **re** means **again**.

Write the word from the word box next to its definition.

reassemble	rearrange	rediscover
reoutline	reconstruct	remix
reheat	recreate	readmit
relearn	reinforce	rejoin

1. To build again _____

2. To put in order in a different way _____

3. To allow to enter again _____

4. To outline again _____

5. To put back together again _____

6. To combine again _____

7. To produce again _____

8. To make warm again _____

9. To get together again _____

10. To find something again _____

11. To make stronger _____

12. To gain knowledge again _____

Name _____

The prefix **im** can mean either **into** or **not**. Use words from the word box to complete each sentence.

NICE ROCKET, DAVE!

improve	impolite	impressed
imply	impatient	impartial
import		

1. Luke was very _____ in his decision to choose Luke's puppy instead of his own for the photograph.

2. Mittens was not a bit _____ as she waited for the can of tuna to be opened.

3. The best way to _____ your piano skills is to practice every day.

4. It is _____ to eat delicious watermelon in front of your friends without offering to share.

5. David's parents were both _____ by his outstanding ability to draw rockets.

6. In order for us to buy products from France, we must _____ them.

7. Eva was not trying to _____ that her rabbit was smarter than her puppy, she was just saying that she was amazed that her rabbit was easier to housebreak.

Name _____

Some prefixes tell how many. Use the prefixes in the word box to answer each question.

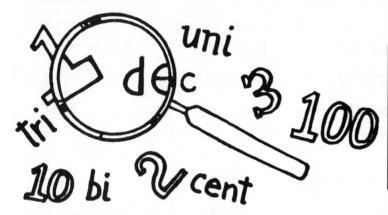

uni	one	**tri**	three
bi	two	**dec**	ten
cent	one hundred		

1. How many years in a **century**? _____

2. How many wheels on a **bicycle**? _____

3. How many angles in a **triangle**? _____

4. How many years in a **decade**? _____

5. How many legs on a **centipede**? _____

6. How many horns on a **unicorn**? _____

7. How many years in a **centennial**? _____

8. How many wheels on a **unicycle**? _____

9. How many legs on a **decapod**? _____

10. How many horns on a **triceratops**? _____

Name _____

Read each word. Write the prefix in the **Prefix** column and the word without the prefix in the **Word** column.

	Prefix	**Word**
1. incorrect		
2. refresh		
3. impolite		
4. mistreat		
5. unreal		
6. subway		
7. astrodome		
8. prewash		
9. unknown		
10. betray		

Name _____

Read each word. Write the prefix in the **Prefix** column and the word without the prefix in the **Word** column.

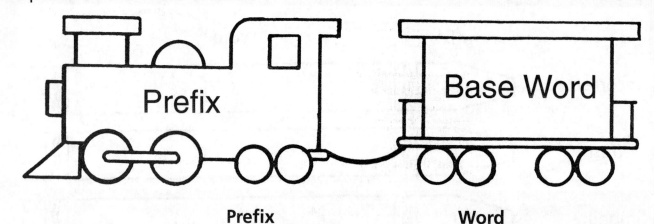

	Prefix	Word
1. midpoint		
2. express		
3. nonstop		
4. disobey		
5. imperfect		
6. infield		
7. unbend		
8. antiwar		
9. telephone		
10. supercharge		
11. belong		
12. incorrect		

Name _____

Add the correct prefix to each word in the word box. Write the new words in the correct column.

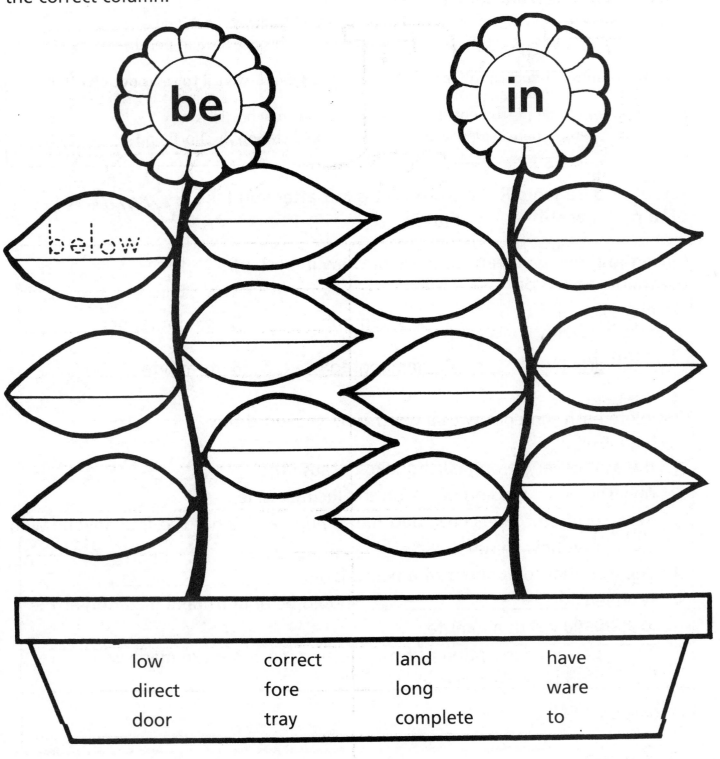

low	correct	land	have
direct	fore	long	ware
door	tray	complete	to

Name _____

graph	to write

calligraphy	the art of fine handwriting
graphic	relating to writing, drawing, or painting; vivid or lifelike
graphite	a soft, black, greasy-feeling form of carbon, used in pencils and as a lubricant
mimeograph	a duplicating machine that uses a type of stencil to reproduce written material
seismograph	an instrument that records earthquake vibrations
stenographer	a person who specializes in taking dictation by shorthand

A **root** or **base word** is the word that is left after you **take off a prefix or suffix.**

Circle the root that means to write or draw in each of the following words.

1. graphic   3. seismograph   5. stenographer

2. calligraphy   4. mimeograph   6. graphite

Complete each sentence with a word from the word box.

1. It wasn't a very strong earthquake because the _____ only showed a reading of 3.1 on the Richter scale.

2. Because photocopiers have become so popular, it's hard to find anyone who still knows how to run a _____.

3. The essential component of a pencil is _____.

4. A skilled _____ should be able to take dictation at the rate of 100 words a minute.

5. The reporter's description of how washing machines are made was interesting because it was so _____.

Name _____

	man, manu hand
manacle	to put handcuffs on, to restrain (verb); handcuff (noun)
manicure	cosmetic care of the hands and fingernails
manipulate	to control or move with the hands; to handle skillfully
manual	done by hand (adjective); a handbook providing information or instruction (noun)
manufacture	to make a product by hand or by machinery
manuscript	a handwritten or typed copy of an article, book, or report before it is printed.

Circle the root that means **hand** in each word below.
Then define the word in the blank using the word box.

Example:
manufacturer   <u>a company that makes products</u>

1. manacled   _____

2. manipulation   _____

3. manually   _____

4. manicurist   _____

Complete each sentence with a word from the word box.

1. After I painted the house, I went to the beauty salon for a
   _____ to improve the looks of my hands.

2. The writer sighed in relief as he wrote the last word of the
   _____ for his novel.

3. Carpentry is _____ labor.

4. The police officer _____(d) the criminal.

5. Roxanne was the video game champion of the school because she could
   _____ the controls so skillfully.

List four manual jobs. _____ _____ _____ _____

Name _____

tele	far

telecommunication	the science or technology of communicating sounds, signals, or pictures by wire or radio
telegraph	a system for sending coded messages from a transmitter to a receiver
telephoto	a magnifying camera lens used to photograph distant objects
telescope	an optical instrument that makes distant objects appear nearer and larger
teletypewriter	a form of telegraph in which messages to be sent are typed out and reproduced by an automatic typewriter on the receiving end

Divide the words into two parts so that the prefix meaning **far** is separate.

Example: television   tele _____   vision _____

1. telescope   _____   _____
2. telegraph   _____   _____
3. telephoto   _____   _____
4. telecommunication   _____   _____
5. teletypewriter   _____   _____

Complete each sentence using a word from the word box.

1. Morse code is the "language" used by the _____.

2. Observatories use giant _____(s) to look at the stars.

3. A _____ is often found in newspaper offices because whole stories, rather than brief messages, must be transmitted.

4. Before the invention of the telephone and the radio, the field of _____ did not exist.

5. The photographer used a _____ lens for the pictures of the lions because he had no desire to get very close.

Name _____

| | un | not | |

Circle the words that use **un** as a prefix meaning **not** or **the opposite of**.

unanimous	unique	unsure
uncaring	unity	untangle
undeserved	unknown	until
underage	unhelpful	unqualified
unicycle	unlock	unwind
uniform	unshaken	unequal

Complete each sentence using a word from the list above.

1. The children were so well-behaved that Jordan felt that the babysitting money was practically _____.

2. If you haven't already studied the material, last-minute cramming for a test will probably be _____.

3. Norman realized that he'd be _____ for a lot of interesting jobs unless he got some computer training.

4. Mona spent a lot of time trying to _____ the knot.

5. The children were _____ about what to get their mother for her birthday.

6. Although the quarter and the peso are nearly the same size, they are of _____ value.

Name _____

mono, uni	one

monogram	a design of two or more letters, such as initials, entwined into one
monopoly	exclusive control by one group of people (from Greek *polein*, "to sell")
monorail	a railway with cars running on a single track
monotony	sameness; lack of variety (from Greek *tonos*, "tone")
unicorn	a mythical horselike animal with one horn (from Latin *cornu*, "horn")
unicycle	a vehicle with one wheel (from Greek *kuklos*, "circle, wheel")
unilateral	of, on, or by one side only (from Latin *latus*, "side")
unison	speaking or singing together (from Latin *sonus*, "sound")

Fill in the blanks with words from the word box.

1. It took many hours of practice before Mike could ride the _____ without falling.

2. To distinguish between the sweaters we gave the twins for Christmas, we had _____(s) put on them.

3. The class recited the pledge of allegiance in _____.

4. After the fourth time he told the story, I was bored by the _____.

5. Without any prompting from her parents, Sasha made a _____ decision that she would clean up her room.

Circle the prefix that means **one** in each word below. Then use a dictionary to write the definition of each word.

1. uniform *(adjective)* _____

2. universe _____

3. monochrome *(noun)* _____

4. unify _____

Name _____

com	together, with

combat	to fight; to struggle against, especially to try to reduce or eliminate
commiserate	to express sorrow or pity
companion	a person who accompanies or associates with another
compare	to note the similarities or differences of
compete	to try to outdo or defeat someone else
compose	to form by putting together
compound	something made of several parts
compress	to squeeze together; to reduce in size or volume

Fill in each blank with a word from the word box.

1. The scientists are doing research to find a way to _____ the new disease.
2. My grandmother has been very lonely since my grandfather died, so my mother hired a woman to be her _____.
3. Green paint can be made from a _____ of blue and yellow paint.
4. The two classes _____(d) against each other in a baseball game.
5. For geometry class, John will _____ the diameters of a volleyball and a basketball.

Circle the words with the prefix **com** meaning **together, with**.

compel	comedy
complicate	complex
coma	compromise
compartment	comet

Name _____

Imported words are words used in English that come from **different languages,** such as Greek, Latin, French, or German.

Below is a list of some English words and their origins.

African	Arabic	Dutch	Hindi	Japanese	Spanish
gumbo	amber	coleslaw	bungalow	bonsai	cargo
jazz	crimson	landscape	chintz	karate	lariat
okra	tambourine	waffle	loot	kimono	vanilla

Write each word from above beside its meaning below and on the next page. You may use a dictionary to help you.

1. a deep red color _____

2. an art of self defense _____

3. a crisp pancake made of batter

_____

4. a one-storied house _____

5. a kind of music with a strong rhythm

_____

6. a yellowish color _____

7. a long, light rope used for catching livestock

_____

8. a printed cotton fabric _____

Name _____

9. a salad made of cabbage _____

10. a vegetable that has soft, sticky green pods _____

11. goods that are transported _____

12. a small drum with loose metallic disks at the sides

_____

13. a bean used for flavoring _____

14. a long robe worn with a sash _____

15. a view or scene on land _____

16. a soup that usually contains vegetables and meat

_____

17. goods that are stolen _____

18. a potted plant that is kept small by special methods

_____

Name _____

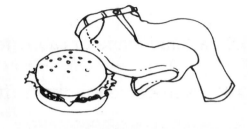

Read the word explanations and answer the questions. Use a dictionary for help.

1. **Jeans** are named for the city of Genoa, Italy, where they were first made. Are jeans usually made of cotton or wool?_____

2. **Spinach** is a vegetable named for the country of Spain. What color is spinach?_____

3. **Cantaloupes** are named for Cantalupo, a villa in Italy where they were first grown. Is a cantaloupe a type of melon or berry?_____

4. A **marathon** is a long-distance footrace. It is named for Marathon, a Greek city that was the site of a battle in 490 B.C. According to legend, a messenger ran about 25 miles from Marathon to Athens to deliver the news that the Greeks had defeated the Persian army. How many miles is a modern-day marathon?_____

5. Fine pottery called **china** is named for China, the country where very fine pottery was made. What is one thing that is made of china?_____

6. **Frankfurters** are named for the German city of Frankfurt. Is a frankfurter made from beef or fish?_____

7. **Tangerines** are named for the city of Tangier in Morocco. Do tangerines look like pears or oranges?_____

8. **Attic** comes from Attica, a peninsula in Greece. Is an attic found at the bottom or at the top of a house?_____

9. **Coach** got its name from the Hungarian city of Kocs. A coachlike vehicle was built in this city in the 1450's. Do passengers sit inside or on top of a coach?_____

10. A dance called the **polka** got its name from the Czech word for Poland, a European country. Is the polka a fast or slow dance?_____

11. **Suede** is a type of leather. The name comes from the French word for Sweden, a Scandinavian country. How does suede feel?_____

12. A **cologne** is a perfumed liquid named for the German city of Cologne. A world-famous perfume was made here. Does a person drink or wear cologne?_____

13. **Hamburger** was named for the German city of Hamburg. Is hamburger made from potatoes or from beef?_____

14. **Indigo** is a type of dye. It got its name from the country of India, where the indigo plant grows. Is indigo a dark blue or a deep red color?_____

Name _____

Complete each sentence with a French word from the word box.

chef	budget	menu
petite	crayon	question

1. The word _____ comes from the French word *crayon*.

2. The word _____ comes from the French word meaning to *seek* or *ask*.

3. The word _____ comes from the French word that means *detailed*, as in a list of items for sale at a restaurant.

4. The word _____ is short for the French *chef de cuisine*.

5. The word _____ comes from the French word meaning *small*.

6. The word _____ comes from the French word *bougette*.

Name _____

Complete each definition with a Native American word from the word box.

opossum	pecan	moccasin
raccoon	toboggan	Canada

1. The word _____ comes from the word for *scratcher*.

2. The word _____ comes from the word for *village*.

3. The word _____ comes from the word for *shoe*.

4. The word _____ comes from the word for *hard-shelled nut*.

5. The word _____ means *white animal*.

6. The word _____ means a *drag made of skin*.

Name _____

Match the imported word with its English form.

_____	1. boss	a.	koekje (Dutch)
_____	2. gopher	b.	koolsla (Dutch)
_____	3. sleigh	c.	slee (Dutch)
_____	4. moose	d.	baas (Dutch)
_____	5. cookie	e.	cucaracha (Spanish)
_____	6. cockroach	f.	gaufre (French)
_____	7. woodchuck	g.	moosu (Native American)
_____	8. coleslaw	h.	otchuck (Native American)

Name _____

An **abbreviation** is the **shortened** version of a word.

Read the words and their abbreviations in the word box.

Sunday—Sun.	January—Jan.
Monday—Mon.	February—Feb.
Tuesday—Tues.	March—Mar.
Wednesday—Wed.	April—Apr.
Thursday—Thurs.	August—Aug.
Friday—Fri.	September—Sept.
Saturday—Sat.	October—Oct.
	November—Nov.
	December—Dec.

Unscramble the abbreviations for the days of the week.

1. tsa _____

2. nus _____

3. onm _____

4. edw _____

5. sute _____

6. rif _____

7. rstuh _____

Unscramble the abbreviations for the months of the year.

1. bef _____

2. mra _____

3. ced _____

4. tco _____

5. rap _____

6. vno _____

Name _____

Write the abbreviation for the underlined word in each sentence.

HS	Dr.	Mrs.	secy.
Jr.	Gov.	Mr.	Mt.

1. <u>Doctor</u> Evans is a heart surgeon. _____

2. Will <u>Missus</u> banks be picking us up after school? _____

3. Mike's dad, <u>Mister</u> Lee, runs his own restaurant. _____

4. <u>Governor</u> Wilson plans to rebuild the old train station. _____

5. My full name is Manuel Javier Rodriguez, <u>Junior</u>. _____

6. The school <u>secretary</u> is on vacation. _____

7. <u>Mount</u> Bluebell is the highest point in our state. _____

8. The local <u>high</u> <u>school</u> made it to the state swimming meet. _____

Name _____

Write the abbreviation for the underlined word on the lines provided.

Dear Micah,

I hope that you are excited as I am for my visit on Saturday, March 7th. I can't believe it's only a month away! Are we still going to the Girl Scout meeting? I can't wait to see all my old friends. It seems like I've been here in California for years instead of only a few weeks. Maybe next time you'll be able to come out and visit me! You might be able to come in August before school starts.

I'll see you soon!
Your friend,
Robin

---

1. _____

2. _____

3. _____

4. _____

5. _____

6. _____

7. _____

8. _____

Name _____

Celsius	centimeter	Fahrenheit
yard	dozen	pound
foot	inch	mile
millimeter	ounces	

Rewrite each statement without abbreviations.

1. 3 ft. make 1 yd.

   _____

2. 12 in. make 1 ft.

   _____

3. there are 16 oz. in 1 lb.

   _____

4. 1 doz. is made of 12 objects

   _____

5. there are 5280 ft in 1 mi.

   _____

6. there are 1760 yd in 1 mi.

   _____

7. there are 100 mm in 1 cm

   _____

8. 32 degrees F is equal to 0 degrees C

   _____

Name _____

A **compound** word is **made of two words** that can stand alone.

Unscramble the given letters and fill in the puzzle with a compound word. Then write the compound word on the line.

1. pieo

| t | | |

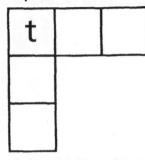

_____

2. aupke

| c | | |

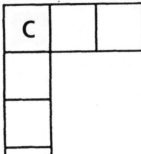

_____

3. hinnue

| s | | |

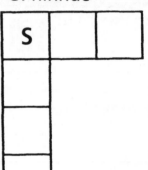

_____

4. eciphap

| s | | | | |

_____

5. htirda

| b | | | |

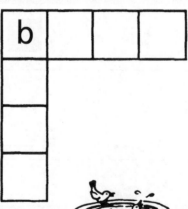

_____

6. ropee

| t | | | |

_____

Name _____

Unscramble the given letters and fill in the puzzle with a compound word. Then write the compound word next to its picture.

1. tcot

u

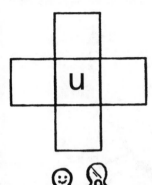

_____

2. ekpnc

a

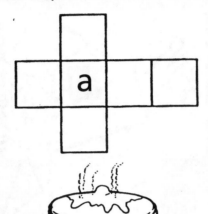

_____

3. llshde

i

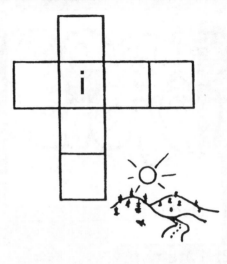

_____

4. whkrme

o

_____

5. llwtref

a

_____

6. bblsel

a

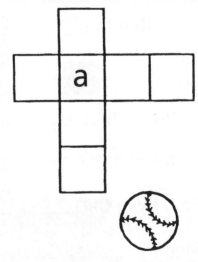

_____

Name _____

Write the missing compound word in each sentence.

sunshine	anyone	fireman	myself	baseball
pancakes	birthday	afternoon	doorbell	airplane

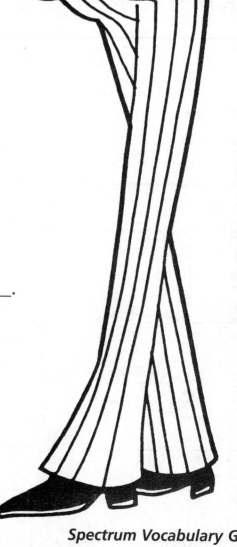

1. Dad is a _____.

2. I ate two _____.

3. Is _____ home?

4. Let's play _____.

5. I saw Kim this _____.

6. The _____ is bright.

7. Today is my _____.

8. I walked home by _____.

9. Let's fly in the _____.

10. Ring the _____.

Name _____

Find a word to go with each meaning.

bookcase	driveway	shoelace	cupboard	doorbell
bathtub	mailbox	bedroom	classroom	doorknob

1. a place for letters _____

2. a place to sleep _____

3. for tying shoes _____

4. a place for books _____

5. for taking a bath _____

6. a place to learn _____

7. use to open door _____

8. place for dishes _____

9. place for the car _____

10. tells you someone is at the door _____

Name _____

Finish the compound word under each picture.

snake	corn	plane	cup	bow
hook	rise	berry	fly	nail

1.
tea _____

2.
butter _____

3.
rattle _____

4.
fish _____

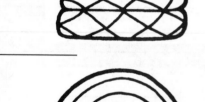

5.
rain _____

6.
air _____

7.
pop _____

8.
straw _____

9.
finger _____

10.
sun _____

Name _____

Match the words to make compound words. Write the compound words.

hand   mother   <u>handshake</u> _____

news   cat   _____

wild   shake   _____

grand   boat   _____

row   paper   _____

under   boat   _____

sail   cake   _____

pan   water   _____

flower   head   _____

fore   pot   _____

fish   meal   _____

day   light   _____

road   net   _____

oat   side   _____

some   body   _____

Name _____

A contraction combines two words using an apostrophe.
Not all of the letters in both words are written.

Write contractions. Cross out letters you do not use.

1. we are   we're _____

2. could not _____

3. he is   _____

4. they will _____

5. I am   _____

6. we have   _____

7. she will   _____

8. cannot   _____

9. did not   _____

10. do not   _____

11. she is   _____

12. they are _____

Name _____

Write two words for each contraction.

1. we'll

2. he's   3. I'm   4. didn't

5. aren't   6. they'll   7. won't

8. I'll   9. we're   10. we've

1. _____   2. _____

3. _____   4. _____

5. _____   6. _____

7. _____   8. _____

9. _____   10. _____

Name _____

WHO NEEDS A HELMET?
MY HEAD IS AS HARD
AS A ROCK!

IF YOU THINK YOU
DON'T NEED A HELMET
YOUR HEAD IS A ROCK!

Write the contraction in each blank.

1. You really _____ ride your bike without a helmet.
   should not

2. _____ signed up nine students to go on the hike
   They have
   Saturday.

3. _____ picked six McIntosh apples to share with my
   I have
   friends.

4. _____ the bird that made her home in the birdhouse
   There is
   we put up last week.

5. _____ be able to play in the band concert next week.
   I will

6. Michele and Mark _____ go roller-skating with us on
   can not
   Saturday.

7. David _____ sure yet if he had enough money to
   was not
   purchase the guinea pig.

Spectrum Vocabulary Grade 4

Name _____

8. _____ going to the library to check out some books.
      We are

on volcanoes.

9. Cindy says that she _____ pet "Herbie," my tarantula,
                    will not

no matter how friendly he is!

10. _____ a wonderful day to go roller-blading!
      It is

11. _____ the book that you wanted to borrow on
      Here is

African animals.

12. _____ all got orange trees in their back yards.
      They have

13. _____ the key that we've been looking for.
      There is

14. _____ ever dive headfirst into water where you can't
      Do not

see the bottom.

15. Jim and Cheryl _____ tall enough to ride on the
            are not

bumper cars.

16. Sue and Sharon _____ be going to see the play.
          will not

17. Steven really _____ jump on the bed like that.
      should not

18. The bus will probably leave before _____ ready.
              she is

Name _____

Write each contraction in the correct section of the snake's body.

1. you + will
2. would + not
3. let + us
4. they + are
5. have + not
6. I + am
7. will + not
8. where + is
9. we + would
10. does + not

11. were + not
12. we + are
13. you + would
14. should + not
15. who + will
16. of the clock
17. is + not
18. what + is
19. can + not
20. it + will

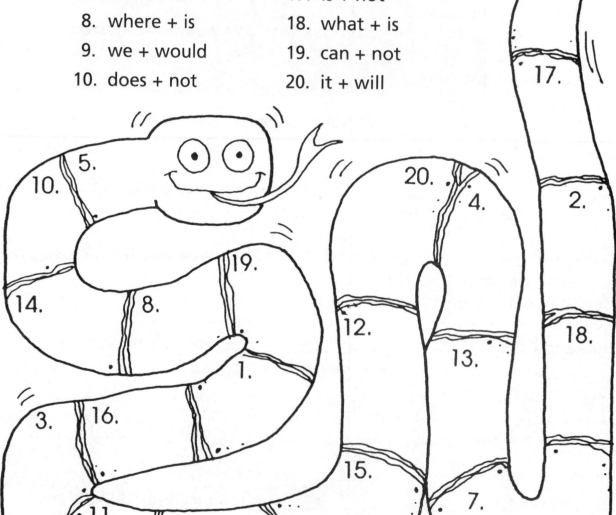

Spectrum Vocabulary Grade 4

PAGE 4

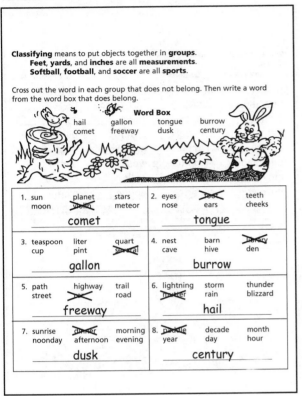

Classifying means to put objects together in **groups**.
Feet, yards, and **inches** are all **measurements**.
Softball, football, and **soccer** are all **sports**.

Cross out the word in each group that does not belong. Then write a word from the word box that does belong.

Word Box
hail   gallon   tongue   burrow
comet   freeway   dusk   century

1. sun   planet   stars
   moon   ~~moth~~   meteor
   comet

2. eyes   ~~toes~~   teeth
   nose   ears   cheeks
   tongue

3. teaspoon   liter   quart
   cup   pint   ~~several~~
   gallon

4. nest   barn   ~~library~~
   cave   hive   den
   burrow

5. path   highway   trail
   street   ~~toe~~   road
   freeway

6. lightning   storm   thunder
   ~~hunter~~   rain   blizzard
   hail

7. sunrise   ~~dinner~~   morning
   noonday   afternoon   evening
   dusk

8. ~~middle~~   decade   month
   year   day   hour
   century

PAGE 5

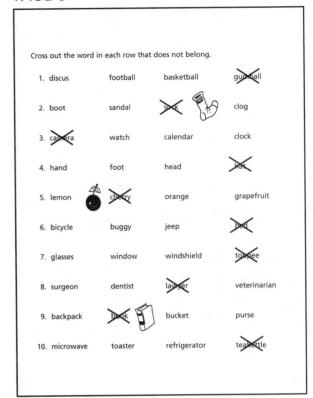

Cross out the word in each row that does not belong.

1. discus   football   basketball   ~~gumball~~
2. boot   sandal   ~~sock~~   clog
3. ~~camera~~   watch   calendar   clock
4. hand   foot   head   ~~hat~~
5. lemon   ~~cherry~~   orange   grapefruit
6. bicycle   buggy   jeep   ~~bed~~
7. glasses   window   windshield   ~~toupee~~
8. surgeon   dentist   ~~lawyer~~   veterinarian
9. backpack   ~~book~~   bucket   purse
10. microwave   toaster   refrigerator   ~~teakettle~~

PAGE 6

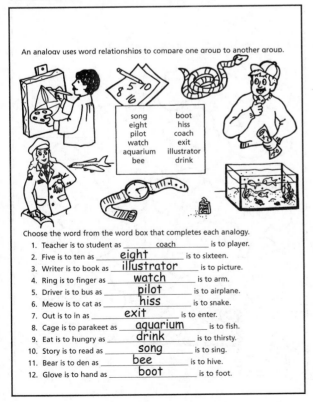

An analogy uses word relationships to compare one group to another group.

song   boot
eight   hiss
pilot   coach
watch   exit
aquarium   illustrator
bee   drink

Choose the word from the word box that completes each analogy.

1. Teacher is to student as **coach** is to player.
2. Five is to ten as **eight** is to sixteen.
3. Writer is to book as **illustrator** is to picture.
4. Ring is to finger as **watch** is to arm.
5. Driver is to bus as **pilot** is to airplane.
6. Meow is to cat as **hiss** is to snake.
7. Out is to in as **exit** is to enter.
8. Cage is to parakeet as **aquarium** is to fish.
9. Eat is to hungry as **drink** is to thirsty.
10. Story is to read as **song** is to sing.
11. Bear is to den as **bee** is to hive.
12. Glove is to hand as **boot** is to foot.

PAGE 7

Classification

Name _____

Write each word from the word box in the correct continent list.

penguin   blue whale   emu   fur seal
beaver   wolverine   giraffe   Canadian lynx
cheetah   moose   koala   orca
hyena   camel   kangaroo   dingo

Africa
hyena   cheetah
giraffe   camel

Australia
emu   dingo
kangaroo   koala

North America
moose   Canadian lynx
wolverine   beaver

Antarctica
penguin   orca
blue whale   fur seal

PAGE 8

Cross out the word that does not belong. Then write a word from the word box that does belong.

nightstand	cupboard	tulips	pen	tools	hat

1. markers, ~~cookie~~, eraser, notebook, book, glue — **pen**

2. bed, ~~penguin~~, comforter, blanket, dresser, pillow — **nightstand**

3. table, chair, refrigerator, ~~X~~, toaster, blender — **cupboard**

4. sweater, pants, skirt, ~~X~~, shoes, shirts — **hat**

5. lawnmower, shovel, garbage can, hose, watering can, ~~tomato~~ — **tools**

6. roses, daisies, cucumbers, tomatoes, ~~X~~, squash — **tulips**

PAGE 9

Write each word from the word box in the correct category to complete the list of foods.

Spices	Desserts	Drinks	Grains/Breads
ginger	apple dumpling	cola	oatmeal
paprika	cobbler	hot cocoa	bagel
cumin	fudge	juice	tortilla
pepper	strudel	cider	barley
curry	truffle	milk shake	cracker
cinnamon	pumpkin pie	wassail	pasta
cloves	eclair	milk	cereal
nutmeg	sorbet	eggnog	rice

apple dumpling	bagel	barley	cereal	cider	cinnamon	cloves
cobbler	cola	cracker	cumin	curry	eclair	eggnog
fudge	ginger	hot cocoa	juice	milkshake	milk	nutmeg
oatmeal	paprika	pasta	pepper	wassail	rice	sorbet
strudel	tortilla	truffle	pumpkin pie			

PAGE 10

Synonyms are words that mean the **same** thing.
Big and **huge** are **synonyms**.
Tiny and **small** are **synonyms**.

Circle the synonym for each word.

ugly	humbly	hasty	homely	hosiery
mean	vicious	vigorous	various	valiant
kind	generate	generous	genius	general
beautiful	eloquent	elevate	element	elegant

Write a paragraph using the four words you circled.

Answers will vary.

PAGE 11

Write a synonym for each word from the word box.

yell	under	small
smile	sick	big
close	help	start
stay	shy	talk
stop	hurry	fix

1 timid — **shy**
2 large — **big**
3 rush — **hurry**
4 ill — **sick**
5 tiny — **small**
6 repair — **fix**
7 scream — **yell**
8 begin — **start**
9 grin — **smile**
10 aid — **help**
11 remain — **stay**
12 below — **under**
13 halt — **stop**
14 speak — **talk**
15 shut — **close**

PAGE 12

Circle a synonym for the underlined word. Write another synonym from the word box on the line.

1. intelligent (bright) friendly — smart
2. assist repair (aid) — help
3. frigid (chilly) weather — cold
4. puzzled mean (baffled) — confused
5. bravery (boldness) frighten — courage
6. dangerous huge (hazardous) — risky
7. easy careful (uncomplicated) — simple
8. trade (exchange) buy — swap
9. repair sell (mend) — fix
10. happiness (joy) smile — gladness
11. calm (quiet) pretty — peace
12. power loud (strength) — force

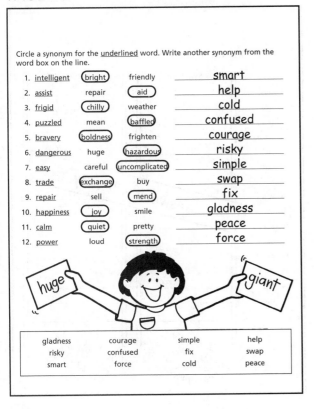

gladness	courage	simple	help
risky	confused	fix	swap
smart	force	cold	peace

PAGE 13

Antonyms are words that mean the opposite.
Big and small are antonyms.
Hot and cold are antonyms.

Look at the picture and read the sentence. Circle the word that does not make sense. Then write the word that would make the sentence true.

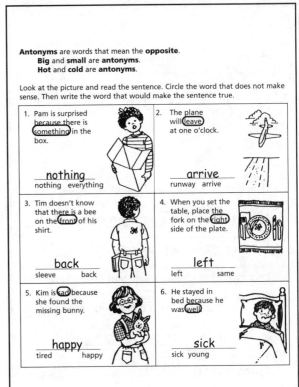

1. Pam is surprised because there is (something) in the box.
   __nothing__
   nothing   everything

2. The plane will (leave) at one o'clock.
   __arrive__
   runway   arrive

3. Tim doesn't know that there is a bee on the (front) of his shirt.
   __back__
   sleeve   back

4. When you set the table, place the fork on the (right) side of the plate.
   __left__
   left   same

5. Kim is (sad) because she found the missing bunny.
   __happy__
   tired   happy

6. He stayed in bed because he was (well).
   __sick__
   sick   young

PAGE 14

Write the antonym for each word.

innocent	present	interior	victory	doubt	rare
defense	increase	shallow	few	wild	plain
departure	minimum	excited	lazy	smooth	rude

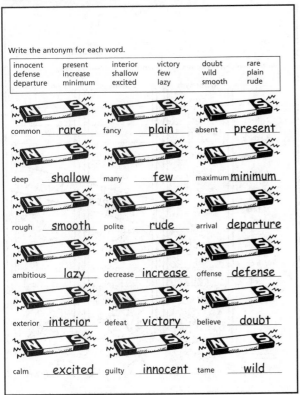

common — rare   fancy — plain   absent — present

deep — shallow   many — few   maximum — minimum

rough — smooth   polite — rude   arrival — departure

ambitious — lazy   decrease — increase   offense — defense

exterior — interior   defeat — victory   believe — doubt

calm — excited   guilty — innocent   tame — wild

PAGE 15

Circle the pair of antonyms in each box. Complete each sentence with one of the circled words.

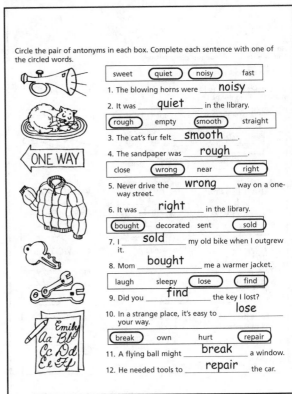

sweet (quiet) (noisy) fast

1. The blowing horns were __noisy__.
2. It was __quiet__ in the library.

(rough) empty (smooth) straight

3. The cat's fur felt __smooth__.
4. The sandpaper was __rough__.

close (wrong) near (right)

5. Never drive the __wrong__ way on a one-way street.
6. It was __right__ in the library.

(bought) decorated sent (sold)

7. I __sold__ my old bike when I outgrew it.
8. Mom __bought__ me a warmer jacket.

laugh sleepy (lose) (find)

9. Did you __find__ the key I lost?
10. In a strange place, it's easy to __lose__ your way.

(break) own hurt (repair)

11. A flying ball might __break__ a window.
12. He needed tools to __repair__ the car.

PAGE 16

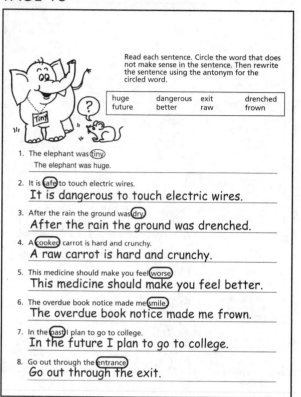

Read each sentence. Circle the word that does not make sense in the sentence. Then rewrite the sentence using the antonym for the circled word.

| huge | dangerous | exit | drenched |
| future | better | raw | frown |

1. The elephant was (tiny)
   The elephant was huge.

2. It is (safe) to touch electric wires.
   It is dangerous to touch electric wires.

3. After the rain the ground was (dry)
   After the rain the ground was drenched.

4. A (cooked) carrot is hard and crunchy.
   A raw carrot is hard and crunchy.

5. This medicine should make you feel (worse)
   This medicine should make you feel better.

6. The overdue book notice made me (smile)
   The overdue book notice made me frown.

7. In the (past) I plan to go to college.
   In the future I plan to go to college.

8. Go out through the (entrance)
   Go out through the exit.

PAGE 17

Write a synonym and antonym for each word below.

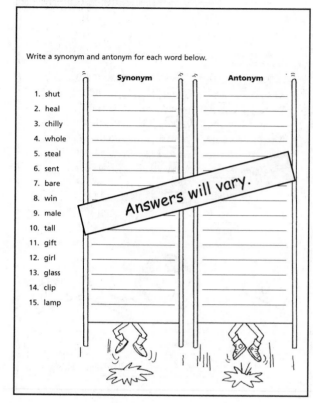

	Synonym	Antonym
1. shut		
2. heal		
3. chilly		
4. whole		
5. steal		
6. sent		
7. bare		
8. win		
9. male		
10. tall		
11. gift		
12. girl		
13. glass		
14. clip		
15. lamp		

Answers will vary.

PAGE 18

Homonyms are words that **sound the same** but **mean different things**. They are sometimes **spelled differently**, too.
Know and **no** are **homonyms**.
Weigh and **way** are **homonyms**.

Use the picture clues to help you choose the correct word for each sentence. Write the word on the line.

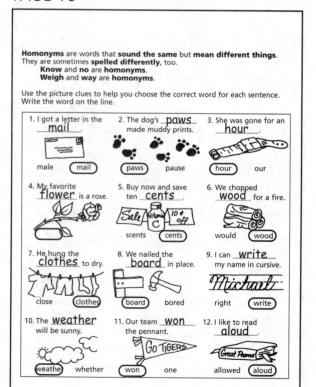

1. I got a letter in the __mail__ .
   male   (mail)

2. The dog's __paws__ made muddy prints.
   (paws)   pause

3. She was gone for an __hour__
   (hour)   our

4. My favorite __flower__ is a rose.
   scents   (cents)

5. Buy now and save ten __cents__
   scents   (cents)

6. We chopped __wood__ for a fire.
   would   (wood)

7. He hung the __clothes__ to dry.
   close   (clothes)

8. We nailed the __board__ in place.
   (board)   bored

9. I can __write__ my name in cursive.
   right   (write)

10. The __weather__ will be sunny.
    (weather)   whether

11. Our team __won__ the pennant.
    (won)   one

12. I like to read __aloud__ .
    allowed   (aloud)

PAGE 19

Write a homonym, antonym, and synonym for each word below.

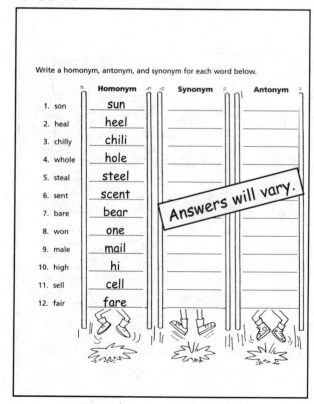

	Homonym	Synonym	Antonym
1. son	sun		
2. heal	heel		
3. chilly	chili		
4. whole	hole		
5. steal	steel		
6. sent	scent		
7. bare	bear		
8. won	one		
9. male	mail		
10. high	hi		
11. sell	cell		
12. fair	fare		

Answers will vary.

PAGE 20

Write a homonym that fits both clues.

Homonyms

nail	well
limb	earth
deck	saw
safe	bill
star	bat

1. where we live / the soil — **earth**
2. branch of a tree / arm or leg — **limb**
3. deep hole with water / not sick — **well**
4. part of a bird's mouth / something you pay — **bill**
5. part of a ship / group of cards — **deck**
6. used to cut wood / had seen something — **saw**
7. not risky / place to keep money — **safe**
8. in the sky / a famous person — **star**
9. on your finger / hit with a hammer — **nail**
10. for hitting a ball / lives in caves — **bat**

PAGE 21

Write the missing word in each sentence.

flee / flee
1. My dog has a **flea** on his tail.
2. Did the cats **flee** when the dog barked?

beats / beets
3. Mother **beats** the eggs with the mixer.
4. Those **beets** are from the garden.

right / write
5. Please **write** me a letter soon.
6. I lost my **right** shoe!

scent / cent
7. I like the **scent** of the spices.
8. I have one **cent** in my pocket.

won / one
9. We **won** the game.
10. I have **one** dollar in the bank.

dew / due
11. The book is **due** on Friday.
12. The grass is wet from **dew** .

no / know
13. Do you **know** her name?
14. There is **no** more candy.

creek / creak
15. Frogs live in the **creek** .
16. Does that door **creak** when opened?

PAGE 22

Read each pair of words in the word box. Read the clues and complete the puzzle using one of the words from each pair.

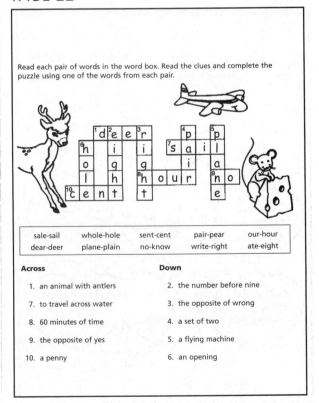

| sale-sail | whole-hole | sent-cent | pair-pear | our-hour |
| dear-deer | plane-plain | no-know | write-right | ate-eight |

Across

1. an animal with antlers
7. to travel across water
8. 60 minutes of time
9. the opposite of yes
10. a penny

Down

2. the number before nine
3. the opposite of wrong
4. a set of two
5. a flying machine
6. an opening

PAGE 23

Context Clues are clues you can find in a sentence to help you figure out what a word means.

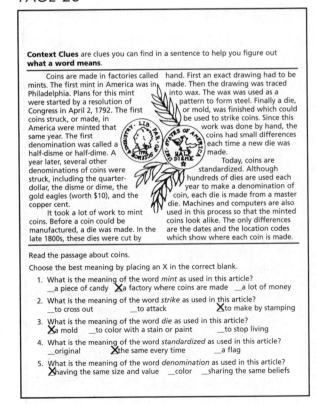

Coins are made in factories called mints. The first mint in America was in Philadelphia. Plans for this mint were started by a resolution of Congress in April 2, 1792. The first coins struck, or made, in America were minted that same year. The first denomination was called a half-disme or half-dime. A year later, several other denominations of coins were struck, including the quarter-dollar, the disme or dime, the gold eagles (worth $10), and the copper cent.

It took a lot of work to mint coins. Before a coin could be manufactured, a die was made. In the late 1800s, these dies were cut by hand. First an exact drawing had to be made. Then the drawing was traced into wax. The wax was used as a pattern to form steel. Finally a die, or mold, was finished which could be used to strike coins. Since this work was done by hand, the coins had small differences each time a new die was made.

Today, coins are standardized. Although hundreds of dies are used each year to make a denomination of coin, each die is made from a master die. Machines and computers are also used in this process so that the minted coins look alike. The only differences are the dates and the location codes which show where each coin is made.

Read the passage about coins.

Choose the best meaning by placing an X in the correct blank.

1. What is the meaning of the word *mint* as used in this article?
   __a piece of candy **X**a factory where coins are made __a lot of money
2. What is the meaning of the word *strike* as used in this article?
   __to cross out __to attack **X**to make by stamping
3. What is the meaning of the word *die* as used in this article?
   Xa mold __to color with a stain or paint __to stop living
4. What is the meaning of the word *standardized* as used in this article?
   __original **X**the same every time __a flag
5. What is the meaning of the word *denomination* as used in this article?
   Xhaving the same size and value __color __sharing the same beliefs

PAGE 24

Use the context clues to help you choose the correct word to complete each sentence.

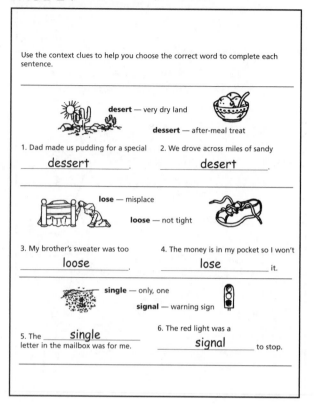

desert — very dry land

dessert — after-meal treat

1. Dad made us pudding for a special
   dessert.

2. We drove across miles of sandy
   desert

lose — misplace

loose — not tight

3. My brother's sweater was too
   loose.

4. The money is in my pocket so I won't
   lose it.

single — only, one

signal — warning sign

5. The **single**
   letter in the mailbox was for me.

6. The red light was a
   signal to stop.

PAGE 25

Use the context clues to help you replace the underlined word with a synonym from the word box.

center	job
lay	strict
utmost	silliness

1.) "I am shocked to the <u>core</u> **center** of my being! What <u>nonsense</u> **silliness** is this when you choose to <u>drape</u> **lay** your wet coat over our precious antique love seat? Be aware that <u>stringent</u> **strict** attention to our museum's guidelines is of <u>vital</u> **utmost** importance if you wish to retain your <u>post</u> **job** !"

crossed	studied
helpful	newsstand
asked	return

2.) We collected a newspaper at the <u>kiosk</u> **newsstand** and <u>traversed</u> **crossed** the intersection to <u>retire</u> **return** to the hotel. In the lobby, we <u>perused</u> **studied** the local page. We hoped to find a movie listing, but could not locate one, so we <u>inquired</u> **asked** at the front desk. The clerk was most <u>contributive</u> **helpful**.

PAGE 26

Choose a word from the word box to replace the **boldfaced** word in each sentence. Use a dictionary to help you with new words.

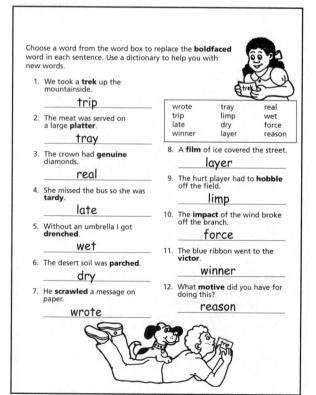

1. We took a **trek** up the mountainside.
   trip

2. The meat was served on a large **platter**.
   tray

3. The crown had **genuine** diamonds.
   real

4. She missed the bus so she was **tardy**.
   late

5. Without an umbrella I got **drenched**.
   wet

6. The desert soil was **parched**.
   dry

7. He **scrawled** a message on paper.
   wrote

wrote	tray	real
trip	limp	wet
late	dry	force
winner	layer	reason

8. A **film** of ice covered the street.
   layer

9. The hurt player had to **hobble** off the field.
   limp

10. The **impact** of the wind broke off the branch.
    force

11. The blue ribbon went to the **victor**.
    winner

12. What **motive** did you have for doing this?
    reason

PAGE 27

Each sentence below contains a **heart** word or phrase. Choose a meaning from the word box. Write it on the line.

center	saddened	courage	loved one	friendly
honest	wanted	from memory	tender	

1. We had a **heart-to heart** talk.
   honest

2. I had **soft-hearted** feelings for the puppy.
   tender

3. It's in the **heart** of the city.
   center

4. I was **heartbroken** by the news.
   saddened

5. I didn't have the **heart** to tell her.
   courage

6. I know that song **by heart**.
   from memory

7. Grandma is a **sweetheart**.
   loved one

8. He gave me a **hearty** welcome.
   friendly

9. I **had my heart set on** the black kitten.
   wanted

PAGE 28

Write the correct word from each pair to complete the sentences.

series / serious
1. We had a __serious__ talk.
2. I've collected the whole __series__.

united / untied
3. My shoe always comes __untied__.
4. We gave a __united__ cheer for the team.

angel / angle
5. The ball bounced off at an __angle__.
6. The __angel__ costume was white.

weather / whether
7. I don't know __whether__ to buy it or not.
8. I hope the __weather__ will be nice.

intend / attend
9. I __intend__ to finish it soon.
10. I cannot __attend__ your party.

lose / loose
11. The knob on the radio is __loose__.
12. I hope you didn't __lose__ my phone number.

accept / except
13. I __accept__ your invitation to come.
14. Everyone was on time __except__ me.

PAGE 29

Read the passage about television. Then answer the questions.

The name *television* comes from *tele-* meaning *far* in Greek, and *videre* meaning *to see* in Latin. Before 1950, the use of television was **rare**. Then, during a single **decade**, the ten-year period from 1950 to 1960, television became a part of almost every household in the United States. It **swiftly** became a **major** influence in people's lives. It changed the way they spent their time and let them see a whole new world right in their own homes.

Since the 1950s television has **evolved**, or grown and changed, to include uses in businesses, hospitals, schools, and law enforcement. As well as providing entertainment, television broadcasts business meetings and **monitors** hospital patients. It lets students study and observe world **events** as they happen, and even guards banks and prisons.

1. Which boldfaced word in the story means:
a. a ten-year period? __decade__
b. quickly? __swiftly__
c. important? __major__
d. grown and changed? __evolved__
e. watches over? __monitors__
f. happenings? __events__
g. uncommon? __rare__

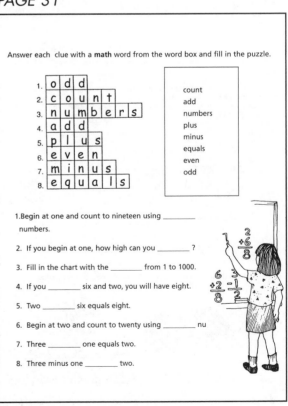

2. Where did the name for television come from?
__It came from tele meaning far in Greek, and videre meaning to see in Latin.__

3. How did television influence people's lives after 1950?
__It changed the way they spent their time and let them see a whole new world right in their own homes.__

4. What do you think is television's most important use and why?
__Answers will vary__

PAGE 30

Concept words are words that have to do with a certain **topic** or **idea**.
Multiply, fraction, and **division** are all **math** words.
Mix, blend, spice, and **bake** are all **cooking** words.

Write each science from the word box in the correct category.

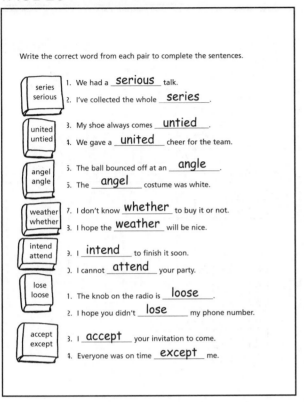

fishing pole, stinkbug, telephone, television, mushroom, laser beam, meteor, toucan, warthog, hummingbird, poodle, aquarium, redwood tree, roller skates, space shuttle, tadpole, crocodile, walkie-talkie

Living	Non-Living
stinkbug	fishing pole
mushroom	telephone
toucan	television
warthog	laser beam
hummingbird	meteor
poodle	aquarium
redwood tree	roller skates
tadpole	space shuttle
crocodile	walkie talkie

PAGE 31

Answer each clue with a **math** word from the word box and fill in the puzzle.

1. o d d
2. c o u n t
3. n u m b e r s
4. a d d
5. p l u s
6. e v e n
7. m i n u s
8. e q u a l s

Word box: count, add, numbers, plus, minus, equals, even, odd

1. Begin at one and count to nineteen using _____ numbers.
2. If you begin at one, how high can you _____ ?
3. Fill in the chart with the _____ from 1 to 1000.
4. If you _____ six and two, you will have eight.
5. Two _____ six equals eight.
6. Begin at two and count to twenty using _____ nu
7. Three _____ one equals two.
8. Three minus one _____ two.

PAGE 32

Use the words in the word box to help you unscramble the animal names.

Across:

3. dhsifrows   swordfish
5. slruaw   walrus
7. ttylfrueb   butterfly
8. aob   boa
13. dkarvraa   aardvark
14. rwne   wren
15. oosge   goose

Down:

1. nswa   swan
2. aierffg   giraffe
4. tteearna   anteater
6. rrleiuqs   squirrel
9. rssoatbla   albatross
11. worc   crow
12. nnuigpe   penguin

penguin
swan
giraffe
anteater
crow
albatross
squirrel
wren
swordfish
walrus
goose
butterfly
boa
aardvark

PAGE 33

Use the clues on page 32 to complete the puzzle.

DON'T USE ANY CROSS WORDS!

PAGE 34

Read this story full of **science words**. Write each **boldfaced** word next to its meaning.

Scientists are looking for new **sources**, or places, to get energy. They are finding new ways to make, or **produce**, the power we will need in the future.

One kind of energy is **geothermal**. "Geo" means "earth" and "thermal" means "heat." Geothermal energy comes from heat that is already stored inside the earth.

Another kind of energy is **solar**. "Sol" means "sun." The sunlight is changed into energy we can use.

1. geothermal   heat from the earth
2. solar   from the sun
3. produce   to make
4. sources   places to get something

These pictures show kinds of energy. Label them **geothermal** or **solar**.

5.

solar

6.

geothermal

PAGE 35

Sensory words are words that describe something you **smell, taste, touch, see** or **hear**. **Onomatopoeia** is a word that **describes a sound**.

Choose a word from the word box that describes each picture.

knock	quack	murmur	zoom
neigh	fizz	ding dong	slop

1. fizz
2. knock
3. ding dong
4. zoom
5. slop
6. quack
7. murmur
8. neigh

PAGE 36

Match the sense with the sensory word.

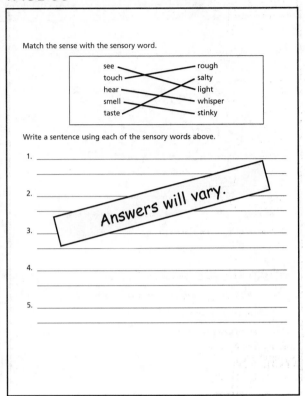

Write a sentence using each of the sensory words above.

1. _____
   _____
2. _____
   _____
3. _____
   _____
4. _____
   _____
5. _____

Answers will vary.

PAGE 37

Rewrite each sentence with at least two sensory words from the word box or from your imagination.

red	shiny	mean
yellow	tiny	nasty
green	happy	excited
striped	silly	relieved
polka dotted	goofy	trusting
brown	ridiculous	confused
mangy	funny	
fluffy	hilarious	

1. I have a sweater.
   _____

2. This is my brother.
   _____

3. Where is my dog?
   _____

4. Did you se_____ ird?
   _____

5. I feel today.
   _____

Answers will vary.

PAGE 38

Fill in each blank with a sensory word.

1. I've been sick for _____ days.

2. That cake is _____.

3. My friends are _____.

4. Can you come to my _____ party?

5. The band is _____.

Complete the poem using sensory words.

I see _____

I hear _____

I touch _____

I smell _____

I taste _____

Answers will vary.

PAGE 39

Read each onomatopoeia word in the word box. Write a sentence explaining what made each noise.

1. drip _____
   _____

2. rustle _____

3. moan _____

4. crack _____
   _____

5. tap _____

6. thump _____

Answers will vary.

PAGE 40

A **plural** word is **more than one** of a person, place, or thing. Remember:
Change **y** to **i** and add **es**.
Words that end in **sh**, **ch**, **x**, or **z**, add **es**.
Change **f** to **v** and add **es**.

Change each word to the plural form.

1. The ___squirrels___ are hiding in the ___ditches___.
   _{squirrel} _{ditch}
2. You will see ___seals___ at many ___beaches___.
   _{seal} _{beach}
3. Put the ___fireflies___ in the ___jars___.
   _{firefly} _{jar}
4. How many ___berries___ did you pick from the ___bushes___ ?
   _{berry} _{bush}
5. Put the ___letters___ in the ___mailboxes___.
   _{letter} _{mailbox}
6. Put the ___brushes___ on the ___shelves___.
   _{brush} _{shelf}
7. I bought two ___watches___ for my ___friends___.
   _{watch} _{friend}
8. We saw ten ___birds___ on three ___branches___.
   _{bird} _{branch}
9. I want two ___lollipops___ for my ___sisters___.
   _{lollipop} _{sister}
10. The ___babies___ are taking their ___naps___.
    _{baby} _{nap}

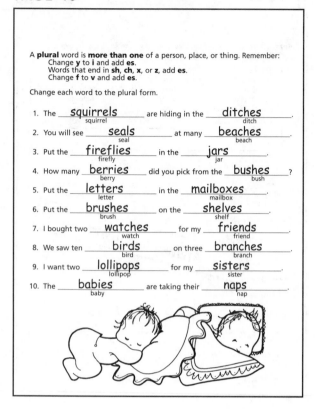

PAGE 41

Make each word plural. Use the plural words to complete the sentences.

1. The two ___loaves___ of bread on the counter smelled delicious.
2. How many ___knives___ do you think a chef would own?
3. ___Wolves___ live in packs and look very much like dogs.
4. The ___lives___ of the ship's passengers were in danger when the storm hit.
5. ___Leaves___ of brilliant colors hung on the tree.
6. The ___shelves___ were filled with a variety of books.
7. All the oranges were cut into ___halves___.
8. The store window was filled with ___scarves___ of all sizes and colors.

PAGE 42

Make the following words plural. Remember to add **es** to words that end in **s, x, z, ch, sh, ss,** and sometimes **o**.

1. ostrich — ostriches
2. buffalo — buffaloes
3. camper — campers
4. balloon — balloons
5. toothbrush — toothbrushes
6. church — churches
7. caterpillar — caterpillars
8. lunch — lunches
9. tomato — tomatoes
10. paragraph — paragraphs
11. skateboard — skateboards
12. volcano — volcanoes or volcanos
13. potato — potatoes
14. class — classes
15. sandbox — sandboxes
16. notebook — notebooks
17. fossil — fossils

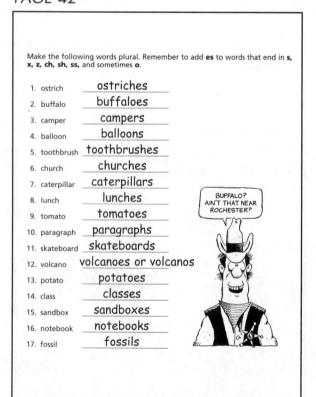

BUFFALO?
AIN'T THAT NEAR
ROCHESTER?

PAGE 43

Change each word to the plural form. Write the word on the line.
Change **f** to **v** and add **es**.
Change **y** to **i** and add **es**.

1. The ___leaves___ are pretty colors.
   _{leaf}
2. We picked ___berries___ in the woods.
   _{berry}
3. We saw a movie about ___wolves___.
   _{wolf}
4. The ___calves___ are in the barn.
   _{calf}
5. There are two ___libraries___ in the city.
   _{library}
6. Dad built ___shelves___ in the garage.
   _{shelf}
7. It costs a dollar to ride the ___ponies___.
   _{pony}
8. The story is about seven tiny ___elves___.
   _{elf}
9. ___Fireflies___ are fun to watch at night.
   _{Firefly}
10. Mother planted ___lilies___ in the yard.
    _{lily}
11. The mother lion has three ___babies___.
    _{baby}
12. The police caught the ___thieves___.
    _{thief}

PAGE 44

A **suffix** is a part **added to the end** of a word. Suffixes change the meaning of words.

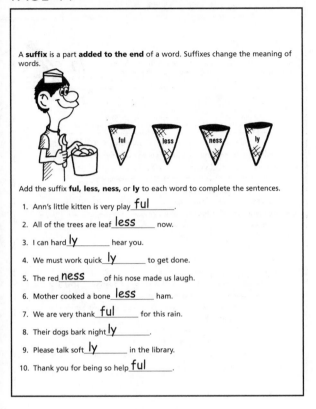

Add the suffix **ful, less, ness,** or **ly** to each word to complete the sentences.

1. Ann's little kitten is very play **ful**.
2. All of the trees are leaf **less** now.
3. I can hard **ly** hear you.
4. We must work quick **ly** to get done.
5. The red **ness** of his nose made us laugh.
6. Mother cooked a bone **less** ham.
7. We are very thank **ful** for this rain.
8. Their dogs bark night **ly**.
9. Please talk soft **ly** in the library.
10. Thank you for being so help **ful**.

PAGE 45

Use the suffixes **er** and **est** to compare words.

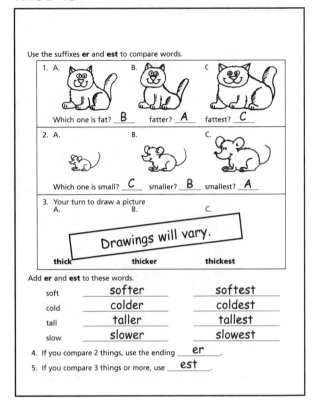

1. Which one is fat? **B** fatter? **A** fattest? **C**
2. Which one is small? **C** smaller? **B** smallest? **A**
3. Your turn to draw a picture
   A.   B.   C.

   Drawings will vary.

   thick   thicker   thickest

Add **er** and **est** to these words.

soft	softer	softest
cold	colder	coldest
tall	taller	tallest
slow	slower	slowest

4. If you compare 2 things, use the ending **er**.
5. If you compare 3 things or more, use **est**.

PAGE 46

Complete the sentences by adding the suffix **er** and **est** to each word.

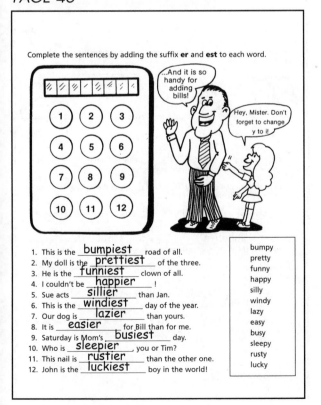

1. This is the **bumpiest** road of all.
2. My doll is the **prettiest** of the three.
3. He is the **funniest** clown of all.
4. I couldn't be **happier**!
5. Sue acts **sillier** than Jan.
6. This is the **windiest** day of the year.
7. Our dog is **lazier** than yours.
8. It is **easier** for Bill than for me.
9. Saturday is Mom's **busiest** day.
10. Who is **sleepier**, you or Tim?
11. This nail is **rustier** than the other one.
12. John is the **luckiest** boy in the world!

bumpy
pretty
funny
happy
silly
windy
lazy
easy
busy
sleepy
rusty
lucky

PAGE 47

Write the word that makes sense in the sentence. Circle each suffix.

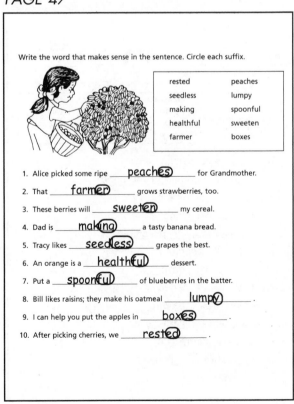

rested	peaches
seedless	lumpy
making	spoonful
healthful	sweeten
farmer	boxes

1. Alice picked some ripe **peach(es)** for Grandmother.
2. That **farmer** grows strawberries, too.
3. These berries will **sweet(en)** my cereal.
4. Dad is **mak(ing)** a tasty banana bread.
5. Tracy likes **seed(less)** grapes the best.
6. An orange is a **health(ful)** dessert.
7. Put a **spoon(ful)** of blueberries in the batter.
8. Bill likes raisins; they make his oatmeal **lump(y)**.
9. I can help you put the apples in **box(es)**.
10. After picking cherries, we **rest(ed)**.

PAGE 48

Add the suffix **less**, **ful**, **er**, **ly** or **ness** to each word. Write it on the line.

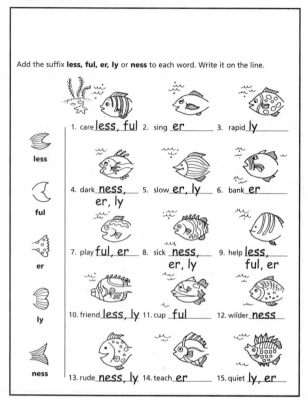

less

ful

er

ly

ness

1. care **less, ful** 2. sing **er** 3. rapid **ly**

4. dark **ness, er, ly** 5. slow **er, ly** 6. bank **er**

7. play **ful, er** 8. sick **ness, er, ly** 9. help **less, ful, er**

10. friend **less, ly** 11. cup **ful** 12. wilder **ness**

13. rude **ness, ly** 14. teach **er** 15. quiet **ly, er**

PAGE 49

Read the suffixes and their meanings in the word box. Then write the word that correctly completes each sentence.

able	— like, capable of	less	— without, lack of
en	— to make	ly	— in the manner of
ful	— full of	ment	— act or quality of
ist	— one who	ness	— state or quality of
ize	— to make	ous	— full of, having the quality of

1. There was much (excitement, excitable) at the art gallery. **excitement**
2. A well-known (artful, artist) was going to put on a painting workshop. **artist**
3. Everyone was in (agreement, agreeable) that the workshop would be interesting. **agreement**
4. People lined up (eagerly, eagerness) to enter the gallery. **eagerly**
5. As the people streamed into the gallery, they gazed in (wonderment, wonderful) at the beautiful sculptures near the doorway. **wonderment**
6. The people were (careful, careless) not to bump into the sculptures. **careful**
7. Some people stopped to admire a painting of a (glamorous, glamorize) movie star. **glamorous**
8. Soon the painter arrived and everyone clapped (loudly, loudness). **loudly**
9. The painter smiled (politely, politeness) and set up his materials. **politely**
10. He began by showing how a person could (brighten, brightly) pictures using just the right colors. **brighten**
11. He also showed how a quick (movable, movement) with the paintbrush could produce an interesting stroke. **movement**
12. When the workshop was over, everyone agreed it had been a (memorize, memorable) art lesson. **memorable**

PAGE 50

A **prefix** is a part **added to the beginning** of a word. Prefixes change the meanings of words.

The prefix **re** means **again**.

Write the word from the word box next to its definition.

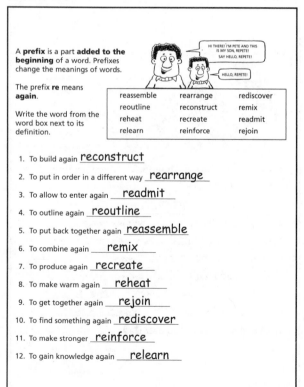

reassemble	rearrange	rediscover
reoutline	reconstruct	remix
reheat	recreate	readmit
relearn	reinforce	rejoin

1. To build again **reconstruct**
2. To put in order in a different way **rearrange**
3. To allow to enter again **readmit**
4. To outline again **reoutline**
5. To put back together again **reassemble**
6. To combine again **remix**
7. To produce again **recreate**
8. To make warm again **reheat**
9. To get together again **rejoin**
10. To find something again **rediscover**
11. To make stronger **reinforce**
12. To gain knowledge again **relearn**

PAGE 51

The prefix **im** can mean either **into** or **not**. Use words from the word box to complete each sentence.

improve	impolite	impressed
imply	impatient	impartial
import		

1. Luke was very **impartial** in his decision to choose Luke's puppy instead of his own for the photograph.
2. Mittens was not a bit **impatient** as she waited for the can of tuna to be opened.
3. The best way to **improve** your piano skills is to practice every day.
4. It is **impolite** to eat delicious watermelon in front of your friends without offering to share.
5. David's parents were both **impressed** by his outstanding ability to draw rockets.
6. In order for us to buy products from France, we must **import** them.
7. Eva was not trying to **imply** that her rabbit was smarter than her puppy, she was just saying that she was amazed that her rabbit was easier to housebreak.

PAGE 52

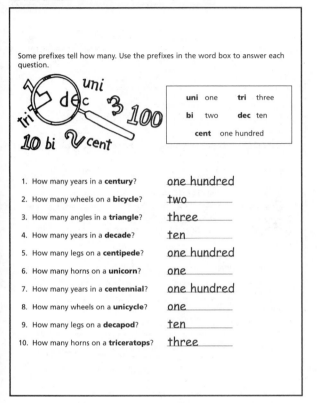

Some prefixes tell how many. Use the prefixes in the word box to answer each question.

uni	one	tri	three
bi	two	dec	ten
cent	one hundred		

1. How many years in a **century**? one hundred
2. How many wheels on a **bicycle**? two
3. How many angles in a **triangle**? three
4. How many years in a **decade**? ten
5. How many legs on a **centipede**? one hundred
6. How many horns on a **unicorn**? one
7. How many years in a **centennial**? one hundred
8. How many wheels on a **unicycle**? one
9. How many legs on a **decapod**? ten
10. How many horns on a **triceratops**? three

PAGE 53

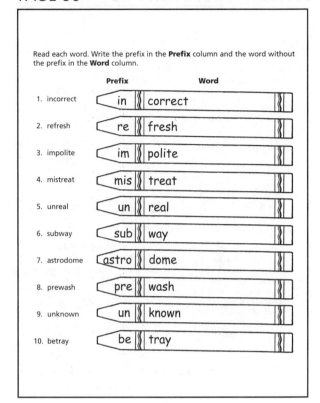

Read each word. Write the prefix in the **Prefix** column and the word without the prefix in the **Word** column.

		Prefix	Word
1.	incorrect	in	correct
2.	refresh	re	fresh
3.	impolite	im	polite
4.	mistreat	mis	treat
5.	unreal	un	real
6.	subway	sub	way
7.	astrodome	astro	dome
8.	prewash	pre	wash
9.	unknown	un	known
10.	betray	be	tray

PAGE 54

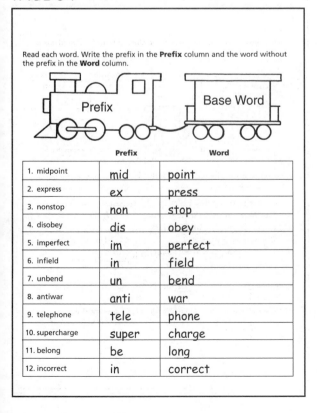

Read each word. Write the prefix in the **Prefix** column and the word without the prefix in the **Word** column.

	Prefix	Word
1. midpoint	mid	point
2. express	ex	press
3. nonstop	non	stop
4. disobey	dis	obey
5. imperfect	im	perfect
6. infield	in	field
7. unbend	un	bend
8. antiwar	anti	war
9. telephone	tele	phone
10. supercharge	super	charge
11. belong	be	long
12. incorrect	in	correct

PAGE 55

Add the correct prefix to each word in the word box. Write the new words in the correct column.

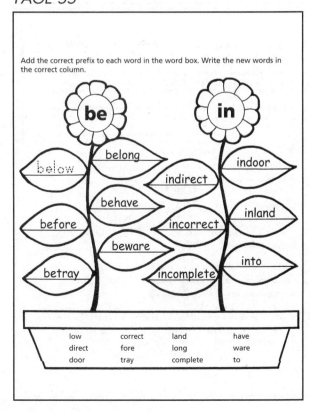

be: below, belong, behave, before, beware, betray

in: indoor, indirect, incorrect, inland, incomplete, into

low	correct	land	have
direct	fore	long	ware
door	tray	complete	to

Vocabulary Answer Key

PAGE 56

graph	to write
calligraphy	the art of fine handwriting
graphic	relating to writing, drawing, or painting; vivid or lifelike
graphite	a soft, black, greasy-feeling form of carbon, used in pencils and as a lubricant
mimeograph	a duplicating machine that uses a type of stencil to reproduce written material
seismograph	an instrument that records earthquake vibrations
stenographer	a person who specializes in taking dictation by shorthand

A **root** or **base word** is the word that is left after you **take off a prefix or suffix.**

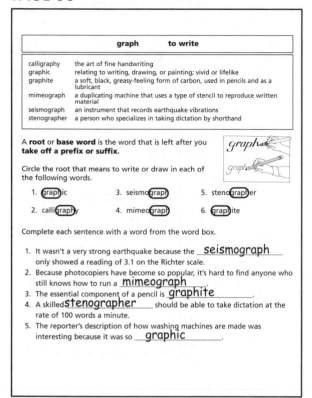

Circle the root that means to write or draw in each of the following words.

1. (graph)ic   3. seismo(graph)   5. steno(graph)er
2. calli(graph)y   4. mimeo(graph)   6. (graph)ite

Complete each sentence with a word from the word box.

1. It wasn't a very strong earthquake because the __seismograph__ only showed a reading of 3.1 on the Richter scale.
2. Because photocopiers have become so popular, it's hard to find anyone who still knows how to run a __mimeograph__.
3. The essential component of a pencil is __graphite__.
4. A skilled __stenographer__ should be able to take dictation at the rate of 100 words a minute.
5. The reporter's description of how washing machines are made was interesting because it was so __graphic__.

PAGE 57

man, manu	hand
manacle	to put handcuffs on, to restrain (verb); handcuff (noun)
manicure	cosmetic care of the hands and fingernails
manipulate	to control or move with the hands; to handle skillfully
manual	done by hand (adjective); a handbook providing information or instruction (noun)
manufacture	to make a product by hand or by machinery
manuscript	a handwritten or typed copy of an article, book, or report before it is printed.

Circle the root that means **hand** in each word below. Then define the word in the blank using the word box.

Example:
manufacturer   _a company that makes products_

1. (man)acled   __handcuffed__
2. (man)ipulation   __control__
3. (man)ually   __done by hand__
4. (man)icurist   __person who takes care of fingernails__

Complete each sentence with a word from the word box.

1. After I painted the house, I went to the beauty salon for a __manicure__ to improve the looks of my hands.
2. The writer sighed in relief as he wrote the last word of the __manuscript__ for his novel.
3. Carpentry is __manual__ labor.
4. The police officer __manacle__(d) the criminal.
5. Roxanne was the video game champion of the school because she could __manipulate__ the controls so skillfully.

List four manual jobs. | __Answers will vary.__ |

PAGE 58

tele	far
telecommunication	the science or technology of communicating sounds, signals, or pictures by wire or radio
telegraph	a system for sending coded messages from a transmitter to a receiver
telephoto	a magnifying camera lens used to photograph distant objects
telescope	an optical instrument that makes distant objects appear nearer and larger
teletypewriter	a form of telegraph in which messages to be sent are typed out and reproduced by an automatic typewriter on the receiving end

Divide the words into two parts so that the prefix meaning **far** is separate.

Example: television   tele   vision

1. telescope   __tele__   __scope__
2. telegraph   __tele__   __graph__
3. telephoto   __tele__   __photo__
4. telecommunication   __tele__   __communication__
5. teletypewriter   __tele__   __typewriter__

Complete each sentence using a word from the word box.

1. Morse code is the "language" used by the __telegraph__.
2. Observatories use giant __telescope__(s) to look at the stars.
3. A __teletypewriter__ is often found in newspaper offices because whole stories, rather than brief messages, must be transmitted.
4. Before the invention of the telephone and the radio, the field of __telecommunication__ did not exist.
5. The photographer used a __telephoto__ lens for the pictures of the lions because he had no desire to get very close.

PAGE 59

un	not

Circle the words that use **un** as a prefix meaning **not** or **the opposite of.**

unanimous	unique	(unsure)
(uncaring)	unity	(untangle)
(undeserved)	(unknown)	until
underage	(unhelpful)	(unqualified)
unicycle	(unlock)	(unwind)
uniform	(unshaken)	(unequal)

Complete each sentence using a word from the list above.

1. The children were so well-behaved that Jordan felt that the babysitting money was practically __undeserved__.
2. If you haven't already studied the material, last-minute cramming for a test will probably be __unhelpful__.
3. Norman realized that he'd be __unqualified__ for a lot of interesting jobs unless he got some computer training.
4. Mona spent a lot of time trying to __untangle__ the knot.
5. The children were __unsure__ about what to get their mother for her birthday.
6. Although the quarter and the peso are nearly the same size, they are of __unequal__ value.

PAGE 60

mono, uni	one
monogram	a design of two or more letters, such as initials, entwined into one
monopoly	exclusive control by one group of people (from Greek *polein*, "to sell")
monorail	a railway with cars running on a single track
monotony	sameness; lack of variety (from Greek *tonos*, "tone")
unicorn	a mythical horselike animal with one horn (from Latin *cornu*, "horn")
unicycle	a vehicle with one wheel (from Greek *kuklos*, "circle, wheel")
unilateral	of, on, or by one side only (from Latin *latus*, "side")
unison	speaking or singing together (from Latin *sonus*, "sound")

Fill in the blanks with words from the word box.

1. It took many hours of practice before Mike could ride the __unicycle__ without falling.
2. To distinguish between the sweaters we gave the twins for Christmas, we had __monogram__(s) put on them.
3. The class recited the pledge of allegiance in __unison__.
4. After the fourth time he told the story, I was bored by the __monotony__.
5. Without any prompting from her parents, Sasha made a __unilateral__ decision that she would clean up her room.

Circle the prefix that means **one** in each word below. Then use a dictionary to write the definition of each word.

1. (uni)form *(adjective)*
2. (uni)verse
3. (mono)chrome *(noun)*
4. (uni)fy

Answers will vary.

PAGE 61

com	together, with
combat	to fight; to struggle against, especially to try to reduce or eliminate
commiserate	to express sorrow or pity
companion	a person who accompanies or associates with another
compare	to note the similarities or differences of
compete	to try to outdo or defeat someone else
compose	to form by putting together
compound	something made of several parts
compress	to squeeze together; to reduce in size or volume

Fill in each blank with a word from the word box.

1. The scientists are doing research to find a way to __combat__ the new disease.
2. My grandmother has been very lonely since my grandfather died, so my mother hired a woman to be her __companion__.
3. Green paint can be made from a __combination__ of blue and yellow paint.
4. The two classes __compete__(d) against each other in a baseball game.
5. For geometry class, John will __compare__ the diameters of a volleyball and a basketball.

Circle the words with the prefix **com** meaning **together, with**.

(compel)   comedy
(complicate)   (complex)
coma   (compromise)
(compartment) comet

PAGE 62

Imported words are words used in English that come from **different languages**, such as Greek, Latin, French, or German.

Below is a list of some English words and their origins.

African	Arabic	Dutch	Hindi	Japanese	Spanish
gumbo	amber	coleslaw	bungalow	bonsai	cargo
jazz	crimson	landscape	chintz	karate	lariat
okra	tambourine	waffle	loot	kimono	vanilla

Write each word from above beside its meaning below and on the next page. You may use a dictionary to help you.

1. a deep red color __crimson__
2. an art of self defense __karate__
3. a crisp pancake made of batter __waffle__
4. a one-storied house __bungalow__
5. a kind of music with a strong rhythm __jazz__
6. a yellowish color __amber__
7. a long, light rope used for catching livestock __lariat__
8. a printed cotton fabric __chintz__

PAGE 63

9. a salad made of cabbage __coleslaw__
10. a vegetable that has soft, sticky green pods __okra__
11. goods that are transported __cargo__
12. a small drum with loose metallic disks at the sides __tambourine__
13. a bean used for flavoring __vanilla__
14. a long robe worn with a sash __kimono__
15. a view or scene on land __landscape__
16. a soup that usually contains vegetables and meat __gumbo__
17. goods that are stolen __loot__
18. a potted plant that is kept small by special methods __bonsai__

Vocabulary Answer Key

PAGE 64

Read the word explanations and answer the questions. Use a dictionary for help.

1. **Jeans** are named for the city of Genoa, Italy, where they were first made. Are jeans usually made of cotton or wool? __cotton__
2. **Spinach** is a vegetable named for the country of Spain. What color is spinach? __green__
3. **Cantaloupes** are named for Cantalupo, a villa in Italy where they were first grown. Is a cantaloupe a type of melon or berry? __melon__
4. A **marathon** is a long-distance footrace. It is named for Marathon, a Greek city that was the site of a battle in 490 B.C. According to legend, a messenger ran about 25 miles from Marathon to Athens to deliver the news that the Greeks had defeated the Persian army. How many miles is a modern-day marathon? __26.2__
5. Fine pottery called **china** is named for China, the country where very fine pottery was made. What is one thing that is made of china? __Answers will vary__
6. **Frankfurters** are named for the German city of Frankfurt. Is a frankfurter made from beef or fish? __beef__
7. **Tangerines** are named for the city of Tangier in Morocco. Do tangerines look like pears or oranges? __oranges__
8. **Attic** comes from Attica, a peninsula in Greece. Is an attic found at the bottom or at the top of a house? __top__
9. **Coach** got its name from the Hungarian city of Kocs. A coachlike vehicle was built in this city in the 1450's. Do passengers sit inside or on top of a coach? __inside__
10. A dance called the **polka** got its name from the Czech word for Poland, a European country. Is the polka a fast or slow dance? __fast__
11. **Suede** is a type of leather. The name comes from the French word for Sweden, a Scandinavian country. How does suede feel? __smooth__
12. A **cologne** is a perfumed liquid named for the German city of Cologne. A world-famous perfume was made here. Does a person drink or wear cologne? __wear__
13. **Hamburger** was named for the German city of Hamburg. Is hamburger made from potatoes or from beef? __beef__
14. **Indigo** is a type of dye. It got its name from the country of India, where the indigo plant grows. Is indigo a dark blue or a deep red color? __dark blue__

PAGE 65

Complete each sentence with a French word from the word box.

chef	budget	menu
petite	crayon	question

1. The word __crayon__ comes from the French word *crayon*.
2. The word __question__ comes from the French word meaning to *seek* or *ask*.
3. The word __menu__ comes from the French word that means *detailed*, as in a list of items for sale at a restaurant.
4. The word __chef__ is short for the French *chef de cuisine*.
5. The word __petite__ comes from the French word meaning *small*.
6. The word __budget__ comes from the French word *bougette*.

PAGE 66

Complete each definition with a Native American word from the word box.

opossum	pecan	moccasin
raccoon	toboggan	Canada

1. The word __raccoon__ comes from the word for *scratcher*.
2. The word __Canada__ comes from the word for *village*.
3. The word __moccasin__ comes from the word for *shoe*.
4. The word __pecan__ comes from the word for *hard-shelled nut*.
5. The word __opossum__ means *white animal*.
6. The word __toboggan__ means a *drag made of skin*.

PAGE 67

Match the imported word with its English form.

__d__ 1. boss   a. koekje (Dutch)

__f__ 2. gopher   b. koolsla (Dutch)

__c__ 3. sleigh   c. slee (Dutch)

__g__ 4. moose   d. baas (Dutch)

__a__ 5. cookie   e. cucaracha (Spanish)

__e__ 6. cockroach   f. gaufre (French)

__h__ 7. woodchuck   g. moosu (Native American)

__b__ 8. coleslaw   h. otchuck (Native American)

PAGE 68

An **abbreviation** is the **shortened** version of a word.

Read the words and their abbreviations in the word box.

Sunday—Sun.	January—Jan.
Monday—Mon.	February—Feb.
Tuesday—Tues.	March—Mar.
Wednesday—Wed.	April—Apr.
Thursday—Thurs.	August—Aug.
Friday—Fri.	September—Sept.
Saturday—Sat.	October—Oct.
	November—Nov.
	December—Dec.

Unscramble the abbreviations for the days of the week.

1. tsa   Sat.
2. nus   Sun.
3. onm   Mon.
4. edw   Wed.
5. sute   Tues.
6. rif   Fri.
7. rstuh   Thurs.

Unscramble the abbreviations for the months of the year.

1. bef   Feb.
2. mra   Mar.
3. ced   Dec.
4. tco   Oct.
5. rap   Apr.
6. vno   Nov.

PAGE 69

Write the abbreviation for the underlined word in each sentence.

HS	Dr.	Mrs.	secy.
Jr.	Gov.	Mr.	Mt.

1. Doctor Evans is a heart surgeon. **Dr.**
2. Will Missus banks be picking us up after school? **Mrs.**
3. Mike's dad, Mister Lee, runs his own restaurant. **Mr.**
4. Governor Wilson plans to rebuild the old train station. **Gov.**
5. My full name is Manuel Javier Rodriguez, Junior. **Jr.**
6. The school secretary is on vacation. **secy.**
7. Mount Bluebell is the highest point in our state. **Mt.**
8. The local high school made it to the state swimming meet. **HS**

PAGE 70

Write the abbreviation for the underlined word on the lines provided.

Dear Micah,

I hope that you are excited as I am for my visit on Saturday, March 7th. I can't believe it's only a month away! Are we still going to the Girl Scout meeting? I can't wait to see all my old friends. It seems like I've been here in California for years instead of only a few weeks. Maybe next time you'll be able to come out and visit me! You might be able to come in August before school starts.

I'll see you soon!
Your friend,
Robin

1. Sat.   5. CA
2. Mar.   6. yrs
3. mo.   7. wks.
4. mtg.   8. Aug.

PAGE 71

Celsius	centimeter	Fahrenheit
yard	dozen	pound
foot	inch	mile
millimeter	ounces	

Rewrite each statement without abbreviations.

1. 3 ft. make 1 yd.
   3 feet make a yard

2. 12 in. make 1 ft.
   12 inches make 1 foot

3. there are 16 oz. in 1 lb.
   there are 16 ounces in 1 pound

4. 1 doz. is made of 12 objects
   1 dozen is made of 12 objects

5. there are 5280 ft in 1 mi.
   there are 5280 feet in 1 mile

6. there are 1760 yd in 1 mi.
   there are 1760 yards in 1 mile

7. there are 100 mm in 1 cm
   there are 100 millimeters in 1 centimeter

8. 32 degrees F is equal to 0 degrees C
   32 degrees fahrenheit is equal to 0 degrees Celsius

PAGE 72

A **compound** word is **made of two words** that can stand alone.

Unscramble the given letters and fill in the puzzle with a compound word. Then write the compound word on the line.

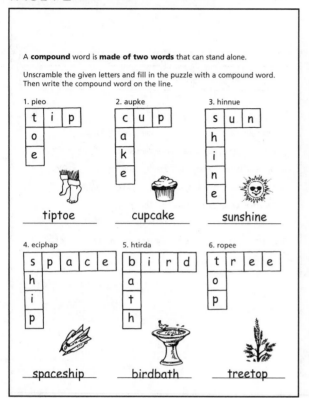

1. pieo — tiptoe
2. aupke — cupcake
3. hinnue — sunshine
4. eciphap — spaceship
5. htirda — birdbath
6. ropee — treetop

PAGE 73

Unscramble the given letters and fill in the puzzle with a compound word. Then write the compound word next to its picture.

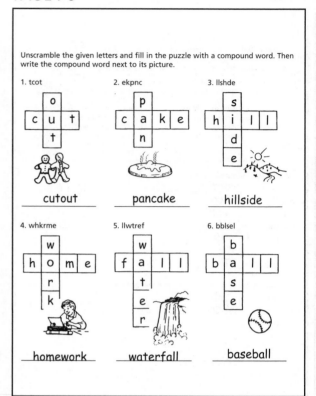

1. tcot — cutout
2. ekpnc — pancake
3. llshde — hillside
4. whkrme — homework
5. llwtref — waterfall
6. bblsel — baseball

PAGE 74

Write the missing compound word in each sentence.

sunshine	anyone	fireman	myself	baseball
pancakes	birthday	afternoon	doorbell	airplane

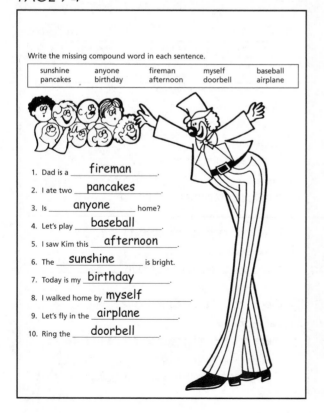

1. Dad is a _fireman_.
2. I ate two _pancakes_.
3. Is _anyone_ home?
4. Let's play _baseball_.
5. I saw Kim this _afternoon_.
6. The _sunshine_ is bright.
7. Today is my _birthday_.
8. I walked home by _myself_.
9. Let's fly in the _airplane_.
10. Ring the _doorbell_.

PAGE 75

Find a word to go with each meaning.

bookcase	driveway	shoelace	cupboard	doorbell
bathtub	mailbox	bedroom	classroom	doorknob

1. a place for letters — mailbox
2. a place to sleep — bedroom
3. for tying shoes — shoelace
4. a place for books — bookcase
5. for taking a bath — bathtub
6. a place to learn — classroom
7. use to open door — doorknob
8. place for dishes — cupboard
9. place for the car — driveway
10. tells you someone is at the door — doorbell

PAGE 76

Finish the compound word under each picture.

| snake | corn | plane | cup | bow |
| hook | rise | berry | fly | nail |

1. tea cup
2. butter fly
3. rattle snake
4. fish hook
5. rain bow
6. air plane
7. pop corn
8. straw berry
9. finger nail
10. sun shine

PAGE 77

Match the words to make compound words. Write the compound words.

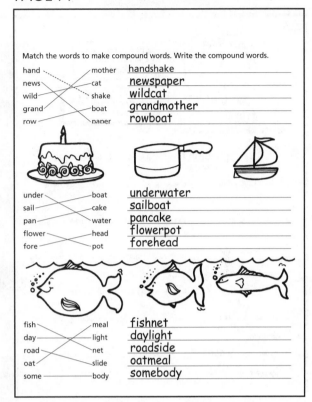

hand ---- mother
news ---- cat
wild ---- shake
grand ---- boat
row ---- paper

handshake
newspaper
wildcat
grandmother
rowboat

under ---- boat
sail ---- cake
pan ---- water
flower ---- head
fore ---- pot

underwater
sailboat
pancake
flowerpot
forehead

fish ---- meal
day ---- light
road ---- net
oat ---- slide
some ---- body

fishnet
daylight
roadside
oatmeal
somebody

PAGE 78

A contraction combines two words using an apostrophe. Not all of the letters in both words are written.

Write contractions. Cross out letters you do not use.

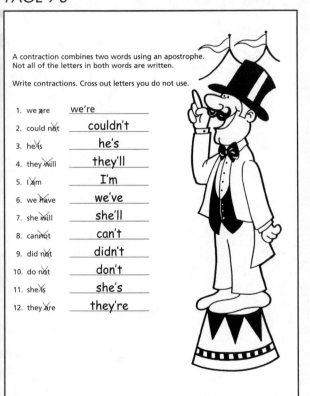

1. we are — we're
2. could not — couldn't
3. he is — he's
4. they will — they'll
5. I am — I'm
6. we have — we've
7. she will — she'll
8. cannot — can't
9. did not — didn't
10. do not — don't
11. she is — she's
12. they are — they're

PAGE 79

Write two words for each contraction.

1. we'll
2. he's
3. I'm
4. didn't
5. aren't
6. they'll
7. won't
8. I'll
9. we're
10. we've

1. we will
2. he is
3. I am
4. did not
5. are not
6. they will
7. will not
8. I will
9. we are
10. we have

PAGE 80

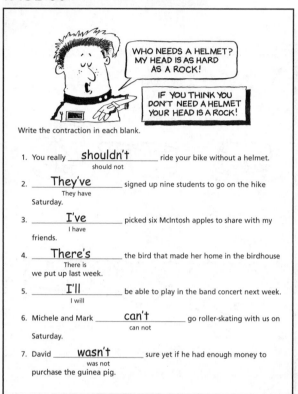

Write the contraction in each blank.

1. You really **shouldn't** ride your bike without a helmet.
   should not

2. **They've** signed up nine students to go on the hike
   They have
   Saturday.

3. **I've** picked six McIntosh apples to share with my
   I have
   friends.

4. **There's** the bird that made her home in the birdhouse
   There is
   we put up last week.

5. **I'll** be able to play in the band concert next week.
   I will

6. Michele and Mark **can't** go roller-skating with us on
   can not
   Saturday.

7. David **wasn't** sure yet if he had enough money to
   was not
   purchase the guinea pig.

PAGE 81

8. **We're** going to the library to check out some books.
   We are
   on volcanoes.

9. Cindy says that she **won't** pet "Herbie," my tarantula,
   will not
   no matter how friendly he is!

10. **It's** a wonderful day to go roller-blading!
    It is

11. **Here's** the book that you wanted to borrow on
    Here is
    African animals.

12. **They've** all got orange trees in their back yards.
    They have

13. **There's** the key that we've been looking for.
    There is

14. **Don't** ever dive headfirst into water where you can't
    Do not
    see the bottom.

15. Jim and Cheryl **aren't** tall enough to ride on the
    are not
    bumper cars.

16. Sue and Sharon **won't** be going to see the play.
    will not

17. Steven really **shouldn't** jump on the bed like that.
    should not

18. The bus will probably leave before **she's** ready.
    she is

PAGE 82

Write each contraction in the correct section of the snake's body.

1. you + will
2. would + not
3. let + us
4. they + are
5. have + not
6. I + am
7. will + not
8. where + is
9. we + would
10. does + not
11. were + not
12. we + are
13. you + would
14. should + not
15. who + will
16. of the clock
17. is + not
18. what + is
19. can + not
20. it + will

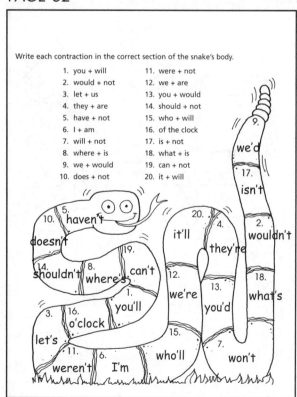

Test-taking Practice is designed to prepare you to use the Vocabulary Skills you've been practicing in the first part of this book on a standardized test.

The first part of the Test-taking Practice is just for Vocabulary Skills. You'll answer questions that test your knowledge of synonyms, Antonyms, Homonyms, and Context Clues.

The second part of the Test-taking Practice is Reading Comprehension. On these pages, you will read a passage and then answer questions about it. The better your understanding of Vocabulary Skills, such as Context Clues, Concept Words, and Root and Base Words, the better you will do on Reading Comprehension, which indirectly tests these skills.

How to Use Test-Taking Practice

Getting Started:
- Read the directions carefully.

- Do the sample items.

Practice:
- Complete the Practice items.

- Continue working until you reach a Stop sign at the bottom of the page.

Sometime during school you may take a standardized achievement test. These tests check to see what you and the rest of your class have learned. they can help you see what your strengths and weaknesses are.

Taking a test can be stressful, but it doesn't have to be! The key is to prepare yourself, whether you are taking an achievement test or a weekly quiz. Here are some tips that can help you prepare for and do your best on any kind of test.

Before the test:
- Find a comfortable, quiet spot to study that is free of distractions.
- Get organized before you start to study: collect all the books, papers, notes, and pencils or pens you will need before you sit down.
- Study a little bit at a time, no more than 30 minutes a day. If you can, choose the same time each day to study in your quiet place. This is good practice for sitting and concentrating for the actual test.
- Give yourself frequent 5-minute breaks if you plan to study for longer than a half hour. Stand up, stretch out, and get a drink or snack (nothing too messy!)
- Try making a study sheet with all the information you think will be on the test. Have a parent, brother, sister, or friend quiz you by asking questions from the sheet.

On the day of the test:
- Get a good night's sleep before the test.
- Plan to eat a light breakfast and lunch so that you won't get drowsy during the test. Too much food can make you sleepy.
- Wear comfortable clothes that won't distract you during the test. If you have long hair, plan to pull it back away from your face so it won't distract you.
- Don't worry if you are a little nervous when you take a test. This is a natural feeling and may even help you stay alert.
- Take advantage of any breaks you have. Stand up and stretch, and get a drink of water or visit the bathroom if you have the time.

During the test:

Be careful

- Listen carefully to all the directions before you begin.

- Read all directions carefully.

- Sometimes the letters for the answer choices change for each question. Make sure the space you fill in matches the answer you think is correct.

- Read the question and all the answer choices. Once you have decided on the correct answer, ask yourself: "Does this really answer the question?"

Manage your time wisely

- Take the time to understand each question before you answer.

- Eliminate the answer choices that don't make sense.

- Try out answer choices in the question to see if they make sense.

- Skim through written passages and then read the questions. Refer back to the story to answer the questions. You don't have to reread the passage for each question.

- Look for key words in the question and the answer choices. They will help you find the correct answer.

- Sometimes the correct answer is not given. Mark "none" if this is the case.

- Skip difficult questions. Circle them and come back to them when you are finished with the easier questions.

- If there is still time when you have finished, go through the test again and check your answers.

Be confident

- Stay with your first answer. Change it only if you are certain another choice is better.

- Don't worry if you don't know an answer. Take your best guess if you are unsure of the answer, then move on to the next question.

- Be certain of what the question is asking before you answer. Try restating a question if you don't understand it the way it is written.

Examples

Directions: Read each item. Choose the word that means the same or about the same as the underlined word.

A surprising <u>outcome</u>	**B** To <u>damage</u> a car is to —
A start	**F** repair
B visit	**G** buy
C result	**H** harm
D meaning	**J** polish

 **Be careful. The letters for the answer choices change for each question. Make sure the space you fill in matches the answer you think is correct.**

Practice

1 valuable <u>employee</u>

    A product
    B worker
    C boss
    D savings

2 <u>tread</u> carefully

    F work
    G carry
    H act
    J walk

3 <u>mistaken</u> idea

    A super
    B accurate
    C erroneous
    D pleasant

4 <u>observe</u> closely

    F watch
    G lend
    H play
    J shoot

5 A <u>jolly</u> person is —

    A sad
    B tall
    C short
    D cheerful

6 A <u>brilliant</u> light is —

    F distant
    G bright
    H tiny
    J dull

7 An <u>accurate</u> measurement is —

    A correct
    B incorrect
    C large
    D difficult

8 To leave <u>hastily</u> is to leave —

    F late
    G quickly
    H slowly
    J early

STOP

Examples

Directions: Read each item. Choose the answer that means the same or about the same as the underlined word.

A To <u>deceive</u> someone **A** hurt **B** call **C** see **D** fool	**B** She had to <u>patch</u> her tire. To <u>patch</u> is to — **F** put air in **G** return **H** repair **J** adjust

If you are not sure which answer is correct, take your best guess.

Eliminate answer choices you know are wrong.

Practice

1 Be <u>uncertain</u> about the location

A not sure
B not happy
C not near
D not aware

2 A <u>coastal</u> area

F near the desert
G near the ocean
H near the mountains
J near the city

3 <u>File</u> papers

A lose
B put in a large pile
C burn
D put away in order

4 The wood was damaged by <u>moisture</u>.

F dryness
G strong wind
H dampness
J great cold

5 My brother was <u>grumpy</u> this morning.

<u>Grumpy</u> means —

A sick
B happy
C unpleasant
D late

6 Who is the <u>author</u> of that book?

An <u>author</u> is a —

F reader
G writer
H owner
J publisher

7 That is a <u>peculiar</u> color to paint a house.

<u>Peculiar</u> means —

A strange
B pretty
C common
D bright

Examples

Directions: Read each item. Choose the word that means the opposite of the underlined word.

A The bowl is <u>empty</u>. **A** full **B** cracked **C** small **D** heavy	**B** <u>original</u> form **F** first **G** active **H** shallow **J** final

Before you mark your answer, ask yourself: "Does this mean the <u>opposite</u> of the underlined word?"

Practice

1 The trail up the mountain is <u>difficult</u>.

    A challenging
    B steep
    C easy
    D narrow

2 Rain is <u>possible</u> today.

    F happening
    G certain
    H not possible
    J predicted

3 That old couch is <u>worthless</u>.

    A wonderful
    B new
    C cherished
    D valuable

4 This lake is very <u>deep</u>.

    F shallow
    G cold
    H large
    J warm

5 <u>recognize</u> someone

    A welcome
    B seek
    C forget
    D hurry

6 very <u>fortunate</u>

    F charming
    G unlucky
    H rich
    J safe

7 <u>available</u> resources

    A inaccessible
    B extra
    C recent
    D active

8 <u>branch</u> office

    F distant
    G large
    H whole
    J main

STOP

Examples Directions: For items A and 1-2, find the answer in which the underlined word is used the same as in the sentence in the box. For items B and 3-5, read the two sentences with the blanks. Choose the word that fits in both sentences.

A | **Please turn off the light.**

In which sentence does the word light mean the same thing as in the sentence above?

A The light is too bright in the bedroom.

B The box was light enough to carry.

C You'll need a light jacket.

D The fire is hard to light.

B Someone bought the _____ on the corner.

A new house costs a _____ of money.

F bunch
G lot
H house
J property

 If a question is too difficult, skip it and come back to it later, if you have time.

Practice

---

1 | **Write a note to your sister.**

In which sentence does the word note mean the same thing as in the sentence above?

A Can you reach that high note?

B This note will explain everything.

C Be sure you note where you parked the car.

D Note how the artist used a mixture of bright and dark colors.

---

2 | **The first batter hit a home run.**

In which sentence does the word batter mean the same thing as in the sentence above?

F A bumpy car ride will batter you up.

G The cake batter is in the large bowl.

H The kittens love to batter each other around.

J Who is the next batter?

---

3 Inez bought a _____ of soda.

The doctor said it was a difficult _____ .

A case
B carton
C disease
D situation

---

4 The _____ is flat.

The runner began to _____ .

F turn
G balloon
H lose
J tire

---

5 What _____ does Carl work?

Help me _____ the box to that side.

A shift
B time
C move
D job

Examples

Directions: Read the paragraph. Find the word below the paragraph that fits best in each numbered blank.

It takes a great deal of ____**(A)**____ to become a champion in any sport. Many hours of practice are ____**(B)**____ , and you must often neglect other aspects of your life.

A	A inflammation	B	F required
	B dedication		G deflected
	C restriction		H extracted
	D location		J expanded

Skim the passage first. Then read each sentence with a blank carefully. Use the meaning of the sentence to find the answer.

Practice

Sometimes the old ways of doing things are still the best. ____**(1)**____ many manufactured fibers, for instance, wool and cotton ____**(2)**____ the best materials for making clothes. Wood and bricks, which have been in use for thousands of years around the world, are the most ____**(3)**____ building materials. When it comes to travel in rugged ____**(4)**____ , horses or mules ____**(5)**____ any machines we have developed. These examples demonstrate ____**(6)**____ that newer isn't always better.

1   A Despite
    B Relying
    C Consequently
    D Before

2   F eliminate
    G support
    H handle
    J remain

3   A unlikely
    B versatile
    C responsive
    D motivational

4   F actions
    G terrain
    H accommodations
    J vehicles

5   A elate
    B deny
    C surpass
    D enlist

6   F conclusively
    G rarely
    H hopefully
    J expressively

STOP

Examples

Directions: Read each question. Fill in the circle for the answer you think is correct.

A Which of these words probably comes from the Latin word *graduare* meaning *to step*?

A grand
B great
C graduate
D ingredient

B The owner had to _____ the puppy for chewing the shoe.

Which of these words means the owner had to speak harshly to the puppy?

F scold
G pursue
H alert
J inspire

If a question sounds confusing, try rephrasing the sentence in a way that is easier to understand.

Mark the right answer as soon as you find it.

Practice

1 Which of these words probably comes from the German word *schnarren* meaning *to growl*?

A snap
B shank
C snarl
D strand

2 Which of these words probably comes from the French word *contenir* meaning *to hold*?

F contain
G continent
H consent
J conform

3 Our _____ visit to the Grand Canyon took place in 1968.

Which of these words means the visit was our first?

A limited
B initial
C sampled
D final

4 Pat was able to _____ the dying plant.

Which of these words means Pat was able to bring the plant back to life?

F elate
G immobilize
H unfurl
J revive

For numbers 5 and 6, choose the answer that best defines the underlined part.

5 farm**er**   build**er**

A place where
B when
C against
D person who

6 **pre**pay   **pre**cede

F after
G soon
H before
J again

Examples   **Directions:** For E1, choose the answer that means the same or about the same as the underlined word. For E2, read the question. Mark the answer you think is correct.

E1 feel grouchy

A pleasant
B healthy
C energetic
D irritable

E2 Which of these probably comes from the Latin word *magnus* meaning *great*?

F magnet
G mangle
H major
J minor

For numbers 1-8, find the word or words that mean the same or almost the same as the underlined word.

1   remain stranded

A crowded
B open
C isolated
D defined

5   If something is withered it is —

A dried up
B soaked
C pushed over
D hidden

2   claim a right

F avoid
G oppose
H solve
J demand

6   Final means —

F next
G previous
H last
J first

3   stitch a shirt

A buy
B tear
C sew
D lose

7   To purify is to —

A obtain
B buy
C confuse
D clean

4   manage a business

F quit
G run
H join
J like

8   This restaurant is very popular.

F expensive
G well-liked
H crowded
J far away

GO

For numbers 9-13, find the meaning for each underlined word.

9 The repair to the bridge is supposed to be **permanent**.

Permanent means —

A temporary
B done quickly
C long-lasting
D inexpensive

10 Your answer is **satisfactory**, so you passed the test.

Satisfactory means —

F incorrect
G acceptable
H long
J confusing

11 The trail to the lake is **incredible**.

Incredible means —

A steep
B extraordinary
C long and winding
D boring

12 The dog was **filthy** after our walk.

Filthy means —

F happy
G clean
H dirty
J tired

13 My cat **crouched** when she saw the bird.

Crouched means —

A jumped
B ran
C cried loudly
D bent down

For numbers 14-19, find the word that means the opposite of the underlined word.

14 **massive** rock

F tiny
G gigantic
H balanced
J high

15 a **brief** visit

A pleasant
B long
C short
D unexpected

16 **guided** tour

F unassisted
G enjoyable
H expensive
J directed

17 I wonder why he is so **timid**?

A frightened
B fearless
C cowardly
D angry

18 The museum had a **formal** luncheon.

F pleasant
G late
H crowded
J casual

19 The package seemed **ordinary**.

A typical
B original
C unusual
D natural

GO

For numbers 20-23, choose the word that correctly completes <u>both</u> sentences.

20 My _____ is running late.

We will _____ the dog for you.

F watch
G clock
H walk
J find

21 This is a good _____ for a picnic.

There is a _____ on your shirt.

A place
B stain
C spot
D table

22 We caught _____ when we went fishing.

The bird is on its _____ .

F bass
G limb
H trout
J perch

23 The officer was very _____ to me.

This _____ of apple is not so sweet.

A nice
B type
C kind
D friendly

24 | Don't forget to put a <u>stamp</u> on the letter. |

In which sentence does the word <u>stamp</u> mean the same thing as in the sentence above?

F The secretary used a rubber <u>stamp</u>.

G A horse will often <u>stamp</u> its feet.

H A <u>stamp</u> can only be used once.

J This machine will <u>stamp</u> the part out of a sheet of metal.

25 | Where is the sock to <u>match</u> the one on top of the washer? |

In which sentence does the word <u>match</u> mean the same thing as in the sentence above?

A The tennis <u>match</u> will begin soon.

B This <u>match</u> will light anywhere there is a rough surface.

C Those two are a <u>match</u> for one another.

D Be sure to <u>match</u> the parts carefully.

For numbers 26 and 27, choose the answer that best defines the underlined part.

26 harm<u>less</u>   need<u>less</u>

F with
G alone
H where
J without

27 <u>im</u>possible   <u>im</u>patient

A too
B so
C not
D of

GO

28 Which of these words probably comes from the Middle English word *fortia* meaning *strong*?

F former
G photo
H force
J foreign

29 Which of these words probably comes from the Latin word *socius* meaning *comrade*?

A sock
B sociable
C solitary
D song

30 The couple _____ to buy a new house when they could afford it.

Which of these words means the couple meant to buy a house?

F expanded
G released
H posted
J intended

31 The ice crystals formed a _____ pattern.

Which of these words means the pattern could be broken easily?

A hearty
B delicate
C denied
D duplicate

Read the paragraph. Find the word below the paragraph that fits best in each numbered blank.

A family of owls has made its home in an old barn __(32)__ to our property. The two adult and two __(33)__ owls spend most of the day sleeping and only become active around dusk. They hunt most of the night, feeding on mice and rabbits. They appear to be __(34)__ flyers, but catch their prey without much difficulty. When morning breaks, the family of hunters returns to the __(35)__ of the old barn.

32 F adjacent
    G distant
    H consequent
    J hesitant

33 A mature
    B capable
    C responsible
    D juvenile

34 F needless
    G partial
    H awkward
    J ancient

35 A occasional
    B security
    C annual
    D partially

STOP

Examples

Directions: For E1, choose the answer that means the same or about the same as the underlined word. For E2, read the question. Mark the answer you think is correct.

E1 nearby store

A busy
B distant
C expensive
D close

E2 Which of these probably comes from the Old English word *seldum* meaning *infrequent*?

F seldom
G insulted
H salad
J similar

For numbers 1-8, find the word or words that mean the same or almost the same as the underlined word.

1 need desperately

A slowly
B urgently
C openly
D formally

2 vanquished army

F beaten
G victorious
H resting
J active

3 investigate a mystery

A look into
B create
C be frightened by
D enjoy

4 gather information

F lost
G distribute
H hide
J collect

5 To be ridiculous is to be —

A sensible
B foolish
C confusing
D pleasant

6 To arrive promptly is to be —

F late
G by car
H on time
J with friends

7 If something is superb it is —

A not acceptable
B worse than average
C average
D better than average

8 You will really enjoy this novel.

F long book
G short book
H long vacation
J short vacation

GO

9 The teacher made a just decision.

Just means —

A fair
B quick
C bad
D unexpected

10 Casey completed every detail of the project.

A detail is a —

F step
G major component
H form
J small item

11 The snow on the mountain gradually disappeared.

Gradually means —

A never
B all at once
C little by little
D hardly

12 Fran felt bashful in front of the class.

To be bashful is to be —

F moody
G shy
H forward
J confused

13 Kayla dismounted and walked around the horse.

Dismounted means—

A got off
B rode on
C ran up
D got on

For numbers 14-19, find the word that means the opposite of the underlined word.

14 monopolize the phone

F use
G lose
H repair
J share

15 lively discussion

A long
B short
C dull
D angry

16 the simple design

F colorful
G complicated
H unusual
J plain

17 a harsh tone of voice

A shrill
B pleasant
C quiet
D rude

18 Ted was definitely going with us.

F possibly
G surely
H thoroughly
J lately

19 Our old car is still reliable.

A dependable
B broken
C missing
D undependable

GO

For numbers 20-23, choose the word that correctly completes <u>both</u> sentences.

20 On which _____ will you go to the hospital?

Have you ever tasted a _____ ?

F day
G date
H plum
J appointment

21 It must feel terrible to _____ someone from a job.

The _____ will keep us warm.

A chase
B oven
C dismiss
D fire

22 You will need a _____ to dig a hole in hard dirt.

Which pair of shoes did you _____ ?

F shovel
G pick
H choose
J buy

23 How long will the play _____ ?

This is the _____ bottle of milk.

A take
B only
C last
D continue

24 | **The children sat on the <u>step</u>.**

In which sentence does the word <u>step</u> mean the same thing as in the sentence above?

F The first <u>step</u> involves cutting the fruit into pieces.

G Don't <u>step</u> on that piece of glass.

H Each <u>step</u> up the steep hill became more difficult.

J The front <u>step</u> was covered with snow.

25 | **The mayor will <u>address</u> the town council.**

In which sentence does the word <u>address</u> mean the same thing as in the sentence above?

A <u>Address</u> her with the respect due her office.

B This is the wrong street <u>address</u>.

C Remember the zip code when you <u>address</u> the letter.

D In golf, you must <u>address</u> the ball carefully.

For numbers 26 and 27, choose the answer that best defines the underlined part.

26 <u>sub</u>marine   <u>sub</u>normal

F below
G around
H since
J above

27 hard<u>er</u>   tall<u>er</u>

A less
B again
C more
D never

GO ▷

Spectrum Vocabulary Grade 4

28 Which of these words probably comes from the Old French word *gentil* meaning *noble*?

F generate
G gland
H gentle
J glisten

29 Which of these words probably comes from the Greek word *phasis* meaning *appearance*?

A fail
B phantom
C phrase
D phase

30 A _____ storm blew down trees and power lines around our house.

Which of these words means the storm was very strong?

F violent
G talented
H pleasant
J subjected

31 Monica found a _____ necklace at a garage sale.

Which of these words means Monica found a necklace that is worth a lot?

A exploded
B exaggerated
C minimized
D valuable

Read the paragraph. Find the word below the paragraph that fits best in each numbered blank.

Young people today have an ____(32)____ future ahead of them. In just a few years, they will see a new ____(33)____ arrive as we leave the 1900s and enter the 2000s. Our world will be a very different place because of ____(34)____ in technology, communication, and transportation. Medical science will ____(35)____ life and let us enjoy active lives much longer. Perhaps the most remarkable trend the future holds is the possibility of traveling to the moon and Mars.

32 F awful
G unkind
H exciting
J opportunity

33 A moment
B century
C guarantee
D sentiment

34 F expenses
G deterioration
H reflections
J advances

35 A prolong
B finance
C adhere
D standardize

STOP

Example

Directions: Read each item. Choose the answer you think is correct. Mark the space for your answer.

The four children sat beside the river and dangled their feet in the water. They had been friends since they had been in kindergarten and did almost everything together. Now that school was finished, they were looking forward to a summer of fun.	**A** **What part of a story does this passage tell about?** **A** The plot **B** The characters **C** The mood **D** The setting

Read the question and all the answer choices. Once you have decided on the correct answer, ask yourself: "Does this really answer the question?"

Practice

1 **Which of these probably came from an ad in the telephone book?**

A The rain began to fall around noon.

B Pablo was sure he could win the race.

C The trout is a popular game fish.

D We guarantee our work.

2 Julian is reading a story called "Voyage to a New Land."

Which of these sentences is probably the first one in the story?

F The family stood on the deck and looked at the land that stretched before them as far as the eye could see.

G On calm days, everyone sat on deck enjoying the fresh air and sunshine.

H I was too young to remember, but my mother told me about cooking aboard the ship.

J It was terribly crowded, with people sleeping anywhere they could find a space.

3 It was going to be a difficult day for the people of Leeds. The huge oak tree in Central Park had been diseased for years, and this was the day it was to be cut down.

What part of a story does this passage tell about?

A the plot

B the characters

C the mood

D the setting

4 **Which of these sentences states a fact?**

F Everyone will enjoy visiting our national forests.

G The prettiest trees remain green all year long, even in the coldest weather.

H The best use of a forest is for recreation.

J Trees supply us with food, paper, and wood for building things.

Example   **Directions:** Read the passage. Find the best answer to each
question that follows the passage.

Pizza has sometimes been called "junk food,"
and in some cases, it really is. When prepared
correctly, however, it can be one of the most
healthful foods you can eat. A pizza contains
nutrients from the major food groups and can
easily be made with reduced-fat ingredients.

**A What helps to make pizza a healthful
food?**

A Using ingredients
B Using low-fat ingredients
C Using high-fat ingredients
D Using one of the four food groups

Look for key words in the question, then find the same words in
the passage. This will help you locate the correct answer.

Practice

Here is a passage about a sport that involves real adventure. Read the passage and then do
numbers 1 through 7 on page 122.

How is this for adventure? Tie yourself into a tiny boat that can tip
over in a flash. Grab a double-headed paddle and set off at breakneck
speed down a raging river. Oh, and don't forget your helmet and flotation
vest. You'll need both, because an important part of this sport is the
guarantee that you'll flip over into chilly water and have to turn yourself
back up. If all this sounds wonderful to you, then you should take up the
sport of kayaking.

A kayak is a small, enclosed boat that was invented by Native
Americans in Alaska and the northern provinces of Canada. They used
these seaworthy craft, which were made of animal skins around a wooden
frame, to hunt and fish in the ocean, but adventurers today prefer the
thrill of shooting the rapids in fiberglass kayaks. Kayaking has grown
today into an Olympic sport that is enjoyed by millions of people around
the world.

The safest way to learn to kayak is to take lessons. Centers throughout
the United States can set you up with an instructor, all the equipment
you'll need, and a safe body of water in which to learn.
Once you get the hang of kayaking, you can rent
equipment and try it on your own in a relatively calm
river or lake. Later, as your skills and confidence
improve, you can move up to more challenging waters.

It is interesting to note that kayaking can be
enjoyed in cities as well as in distant mountain rivers.
Even in the large cities in the East, like New York,
Philadelphia, and Washington, DC, kayakers are
having a ball in local rivers and even the runoff
created by heavy storms.

GO⟩

1   The kayak was invented by —

   A   Canadians.

   B   modern adventurers.

   C   residents of cities in the East.

   D   Native Americans.

2   Most kayaks today are made of

   F   animal skins.

   G   fiberglass.

   H   wood.

   J   aluminum.

3   Which of these would be the best title
     for the passage?

   A   "The Double Paddle"

   B   "Adventure in the Ocean"

   C   "River Fun"

   D   "Old Boat, New Adventure"

4   What does the author mean by the
     phrase "shooting the rapids"?

   F   Shooting quickly

   G   Riding a kayak in ocean waves

   H   Riding a kayak down river rapids

   J   Hunting from a kayak

5   When you kayak down a river, you can
     almost always expect to —

   A   be pushed off course by strong winds or
       ocean currents.

   B   get turned upside-down in the water.

   C   risk going over a waterfall.

   D   lose equipment like paddles, helmets, or
       flotation vests.

6   Which paragraph from the story best
     supports your answer for number 5?

   F   Paragraph 1
   G   Paragraph 2
   H   Paragraph 3
   J   Paragraph 4

7   The story suggests that once you have
     learned the basics, you can kayak in
     more challenging waters.

   A word that means the **opposite of**
   challenging is —

   A   difficult.

   B   deep.

   C   easy.

   D   violent.

GO

Spectrum Vocabulary Grade 4

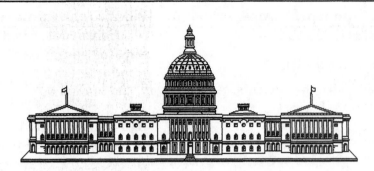

Mr. Madison's fourth grade class would be leaving soon for their trip to the state capitol. Every year Mr. Madison went through the same preparations and wondered if the weeklong trip each spring was really worth all the work that went into it.

At the beginning of the school year, Mr. Madison talked to his students about the trip and showed them photographs and videos of the fourth grade trip from the year before. He met with the parents of his students to get them involved with planning the trip. He also wanted the parents to have plenty of time to save money for the trip in the spring or to help their son or daughter earn the money needed.

The class would begin immediately to hold car washes, cake sales, and spaghetti dinners to raise money. Everyone in the class was expected to work on at least one project. Mr. Madison and some of the parents found businesses and other people in the community who thought the trip to the state capitol was a good idea. They would be sponsors and donate money to help pay for many of the costs of the trip, such as hiring the bus that would take the class to the state capitol and renting rooms at a nearby hotel.

During the school year, the fourth grade would be learning more about the history of their state. When they went to the capitol in the spring, they would visit some of the places they had learned about and see how their state government worked. But that wasn't all they would do. They would take a ride on a subway, visit an aquarium, go to a skating rink, and even see a major league baseball game. Mr. Madison wanted his students to experience many things that were not available in their small town. He also planned so many activities into each of the four days that everyone would be very tired at the end of each day. Mr. Madison wanted his students to be too exhausted to be thinking up mischief in the middle of the night.

GO▷

8 In this passage, "sponsors" were people or organizations that —

   F contributed money for the trip.

   G went to the capitol with the students.

   H rented the bus to the students.

   J had offices in the capitol.

9 Why did Mr. Madison plan so many activities for each day of the trip?

   A So the students wouldn't want to eat too many meals

   B To keep the students from getting into trouble at night

   C To save money by buying group tickets

   D So the sponsors would think the students had a good time

10 Mr. Madison must have thought the trip to the capitol —

   F was not worth all the effort.

   G was easy to plan because he had done it before.

   H was hard to plan because there were so many students.

   J was worth all the effort.

11 What is the main reason that Mr. Madison took his class to the state capitol each year?

   A So they would learn more than just what was in their books

   B As a reward for the hard work the students did all year

   C So parents would have a chance to raise money for the trip

   D So the students could find sponsors for the trip

12 What does the passage say about where the students lived?

   F It was a large city.

   G It was a small town.

   H It was a suburb of a large city.

   J Even though it was a small town, it was the state capitol.

13 Why was the class trip held in the spring?

   A The capitol was busier at other times of the year

   B The weather in the spring was better than any other time of year

   C The students would have most of the school year to prepare for it

   D It gave the students a chance to study for final exams

Example   **Directions:** Read the passage. Find the best answer to each
question that follows the passage.

Gabby couldn't wait for her parents to get home. They were at the computer store, and she hoped they would bring one home for her. She had asked for a computer often, but the family just couldn't afford one. When her father got a new job, the first thing he did was promise he would get a computer for the children.	**A** **How will Gabby feel if her parents don't come home with a computer?** **A** Angry **B** Disappointed **C** Pleased **D** Confused

Skim the passage then read the questions. Refer back to the passage to find the answers. You don't have to reread the story for each question.

Practice

Here is a passage about someone who did a remarkable deed. Read the passage and then do numbers 1 through 6 on page 126.

The Hero

Michael hated the building he lived in. His family's apartment was clean and nice inside, but the outside was dirty and run-down. Trash was everywhere, and all the buildings needed to be painted. He wished his family could move. Michael wasn't happy sharing a room with his little brother. Joey whined and cried. He had to go to bed early, and Michael could not do homework or read in their room. Joey wanted Michael to play with him, and Michael wanted to go outside with his friends. He heard some neighbors say that someone ought to just set fire to this old building, it was so bad.

One night Michael dreamed that he smelled smoke. He woke up and realized it was no dream. The building was on fire. He had to climb out the window and save himself. He heard Joey cry out in his sleep. He heard his father's voice saying, "The fire is in the hall. I can't get to them!"

Michael knew what he had to do. He grabbed some blankets and wrapped Joey in them. Joey started to cry and call out his name. Michael talked to Joey and told him not to be afraid. He carefully climbed out of the burning building and made his way over to the fire escape with the heavy child in his arms.

When they got to the ground, people were crying and screaming. Michael handed his brother to a firefighter and sat down on the ground. He felt very alone and very afraid. Just then his mother and father came up to the boys and cried and hugged them both. "We thought you were gone. We couldn't get down the hall," their father said. "Michael, you are a hero for saving your brother's life."

GO

Michael didn't want to be a hero. He wanted his old apartment back. He wanted his books and toys. He knew how much danger there had been. What if he hadn't been able to get Joey out? Michael didn't feel good at all.

Just then, Michael looked up into the brightest light he had ever seen. A fireman was holding Joey, and a television newswoman was asking Michael how it felt to be a hero. "I don't know," Michael answered quietly. "I just wanted to save my brother."

When the newswoman talked to Michael's parents, they said they didn't care about their things, as long as their boys were all right. They looked at the boys, and Michael looked at his little brother. He knew he had many reasons to feel good about what he had done.

1 **Which of these is an *opinion* in the story?**

A Joey changed and did not whine and cry any more.

B Michael and several of his neighbors did not like the place they lived.

C Michael's parents tried to save the boys.

D Michael was on the television news.

2 **You can tell from the story that Michael—**

F really loved his brother.

G was selfish.

H was a coward.

J was a good student in school.

3 **At the end of the story, Michael felt—**

A happy.

B angry.

C ashamed.

D afraid.

4 **This story was probably written to tell about—**

F why fire is dangerous.

G how apartment neighbors got a new home.

H how a person did what he had to do.

J why little brothers can be pests.

5 **The first paragraph—**

A explains how the fire started.

B tells about Michael and his brother.

C describes the furniture in the room.

D introduces Michael's parents.

6 **Michael didn't want to play with Joey because—**

F he had to do schoolwork instead.

G Joey always wanted to play the same games.

H he didn't like Joey very much.

J he wanted to play with his friends instead.

GO

Spectrum Vocabulary Grade 4

"Max, get off the couch!" yelled Andy as he and his cousin, Jake, came into the living room.

The big-eared dog opened his eyes and studied the boys for a moment before letting out a long sigh and closing his eyes again.

"MAX!" yelled Andy even louder than before. "GET OFF THE COUCH!"

Max's ears perked up and he opened his eyes, but he stayed in the same spot on the couch watching first one boy and then the other.

"Look, Max, if you get off the couch, I'll get you a dog treat," promised Andy.

Max's tail thumped against the couch, but he didn't move at all.

"Andy, you really have a problem with your dog," said Jake. "He hasn't learned who is the alpha dog in this house."

"What's an alpha dog, Jake? Is that anything like an alphabet?" Andy asked with a grin.

"Well sort of, but you really have to understand how dogs think in order to get them to do what you want. Dogs are members of the same animal family as wolves. Wolves hunt and travel in packs, following a lead wolf who is the strongest male in the pack. When two wolves or dogs meet, the weaker one may lie down and offer his throat. This tells the stronger animal the other one doesn't want to fight. The strongest animal in the pack is known as the alpha, like the letter A. The next strongest is the beta, or letter B, and so on down the line to the weakest animal in the pack," explained Jake.

GO

7 This story web is about the story. Which box contains information that does not belong?

A Box 1

B Box 2

C Box 3

D Box 4

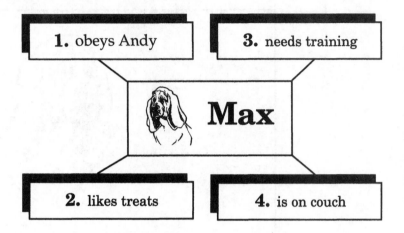

1. obeys Andy

3. needs training

Max

2. likes treats

4. is on couch

8 The main problem with Max was that he —

F only followed commands when he was rewarded.

G couldn't hear Andy's commands so he ignored them.

H was unfriendly to people.

J was on the couch.

9 How does a weaker dog show a stronger dog it doesn't want to fight?

A By barking quietly

B By running away

C By growling then running away

D By appearing defenseless

10 What did Max do when Andy yelled at him?

F He became frightened.

G He jumped off the couch.

H He just looked at Andy.

J He growled at Andy.

11 How can Andy get Max to do as he is told?

A Convince Max that Andy will growl at him

B Convince Max that Andy is the alpha dog

C Make him lie down

D Make Max the alpha dog

12 How does Andy feel when Max won't get off the couch?

F Sad

G Frustrated

H Disappointed

J Worried

13 What happens in a pack of wolves if the alpha wolf disappears?

A An alpha wolf from another pack becomes the leader.

B The wolves fight among themselves.

C The beta wolf becomes the leader.

D The pack also disappears.

GO

Unexpected Visitors

It was a chilly spring morning when Raymond got the surprise of his life. He went outside to put a bag of trash in the can when he saw three bears around the bird feeder. Without thinking, he dropped the bag of trash and rushed back into the house.

"Mom! Dad! Come quick. There are bears outside. They are eating the birdseed. Hurry! What shall we do?"

Raymond's parents rushed to the window and looked outside. Sure enough, a mother bear and her two cubs were nibbling at the birdseed around the ground under the feeder. They seemed quite content and were having a wonderful breakfast.

Just then, Raymond's sisters came down. They looked out the window and jumped back behind their parents.

"Aren't bears dangerous?" asked Merri.

"Not really," answered her mother. "They are shy animals and will usually run away as soon as they know people are around."

"Then why are they so close to the house?" It was Hannah, the youngest sister, and she sounded worried.

"They can't see us," said Mr. Turner. "The bears are just doing what comes naturally, looking for food. The bird seed is a real treat for them."

Just then the mother bear stood up and gave the bird feeder a whack with her paw. The top popped off and all the seeds inside spilled to the ground. The two cubs and the mother began gobbling up the seeds.

"So much for that bird feeder," commented Mrs. Turner.

"It was an old one, and we can buy another. The feed store has a new type that is bearproof. We can hang it higher so the bears can't reach it. I don't mind losing the feeder to the bears this time. How many people in New Jersey get to see bears in their backyard?"

The family stood at the window for a few minutes, watching the bears. They finished up the seed and looked around for other things to eat. Finding nothing, the mother bear made a growling sound and started walking off. The two cubs followed her, tumbling over one another playfully, but always keeping up with the mother. In a moment, they disappeared into the woods.

"Boy," giggled Raymond, "am I going to have a great story for the kids in school!"

14 **In this story, Hannah sounds —**

   F disappointed.

   G excited.

   H angry.

   J concerned.

15 **Which of these events will most likely happen after the end of this story?**

   A Raymond will burn the trash.

   B Hannah will always be afraid of bears and other animals.

   C Raymond will pick up the bag of trash he dropped.

   D Merri will write a story about the bears.

16 **How did the mother bear signal to the cubs?**

   F By picking them up in her mouth

   G By growling

   H By sniffing at them

   J By licking them

17 **From this story, you learn that —**

   A bears and people are afraid of one another.

   B bears aren't afraid of people.

   C people aren't afraid of bears.

   D bears are afraid of houses.

18 **This story is mostly about —**

   F the life of bears.

   G an unexpected encounter.

   H what bears eat.

   J a boy getting ready for school.

19 **From this story, you can conclude that —**

   A bears are seen by many people in New Jersey.

   B bears and birds are enemies.

   C Mr. Turner was angry that the bear damaged the bird feeder.

   D not many people in New Jersey see bears in their backyard.

20 **When Raymond tells this story to his friends at school, they will probably —**

   F believe him right away because this is a common happening.

   G go home and look for bears at their own bird feeders.

   H doubt it really happened to him because the story is unusual.

   J doubt any other story Raymond tries to tell them.

It was a bright, sunny day, and Rosa was enjoying the beach with her family. Early in the afternoon, however, clouds began building up in the west. Soon they had moved closer and a cool wind started blowing. Mr. Gomez suggested that the family get everything together in case they had to leave quickly.

A Mr. Gomez wanted everyone to get ready because —

A it was getting too hot.
B the beach was crowded.
C he expected a storm.
D the water was too cold.

Read the title to the story and then the story. Read each question on the next page and choose the answer you think is best. Mark the space for your answer.

Weather Makers

Our earth is often surrounded by clouds. If we could look down from a spaceship, we would see bands of gray streaks and mounds that look like fluffy cotton. Some might be like thin strips of spider webs.

The clouds that usually bring rain are called nimbus clouds. They are large and dark, and often rise high into the sky.

The wispy, light clouds that appear very high in the sky are called cirrus clouds. Sometimes called horsetails, they appear when the weather is about to change from fair to stormy.

Cumulus clouds are large, white, and puffy, and look very much like cotton balls. They appear on fair days, but can sometimes form thunderheads on hot, moist days.

Clouds are made up of water vapor. They form when water on the earth evaporates and changes to a gas in the air. This water comes from lakes, rivers, and oceans. When the water vapor rises to where it cools, it mixes with tiny pieces of dust to form clouds.

As the water vapor in the clouds rises higher, it gets cooler. The higher it gets, the cooler it gets. When the water vapor cools down enough, the cloud gives up some of its water. Cooler air cannot hold as much water as warm air, so the water falls back to earth in the form of rain.

Clouds protect the earth in two ways. In the summer, clouds help keep the temperature cooler. In the winter, clouds help keep the earth warmer. Summer days are hotter when there are no clouds. Winter days are colder when there are no clouds. Clouds act like a blanket over the earth. Clouds keep the water moving from earth to sky and back to earth again. By "making weather," clouds help keep the earth from becoming too wet or too dry and too hot or too cold.

GO

1   **If the writer were to add to this story, which of these would fit best?**

   A   How a plane flew into a cloud and an adventure started

   B   Artists who liked to draw clouds

   C   Making decorative clouds with cotton

   D   How people can seed clouds to make it rain

2   **After water vapor rises from the earth and forms clouds, what happens next?**

   F   The air on earth gets cooler.

   G   Lightning and thunder appear several hours later.

   H   Clouds rise higher, become cooler, and dump rain back on earth.

   J   The air on earth gets warmer.

3   **Clouds are mostly —**

   A   dust.

   B   blowing snow.

   C   water vapor.

   D   foam.

4   **After reading the passage, you might compare clouds to —**

   F   using an umbrella for shade.

   G   filling a bucket of water.

   H   watering a lawn.

   J   climbing a tall tree.

5   **If there were no clouds, the earth would be —**

   A   warmer in winter and cooler in summer.

   B   cooler in winter and warmer in summer.

   C   warmer all the time.

   D   cooler all the time.

6   **The fifth paragraph is mainly about —**

   F   how clouds are formed.

   G   why clouds are important on the earth.

   H   what clouds look like.

   J   what causes fog.

GO

Spectrum Vocabulary Grade 4

Speedy Makes a Friend

"This looks like a safe place," Speedy said to himself. Then he scurried under the barn and looked around a bit. He had been in his family's nest in a field when a farmer started plowing the ground. All the rabbits ran in different directions. Speedy didn't even know where the others were, but he was almost grown anyway. He was ready to go out on his own and live his own life.

Right outside the barn was a nice vegetable garden. Green plants were lined up in rows, so he would have plenty to eat. Beside the garden was a nice lawn with delicious grass. Speedy had just stepped out from under the barn to visit the garden when he saw an enormous, black dog. He was so scared that he dove under the barn as fast as he could. The dog, however, did not growl or chase him. The next day he let the dog see him, but stayed close to the barn. Then he slowly hopped out, and the dog did not seem to care about him at all. Speedy felt safe. He even drank water from the big dog's dish, but only when the dog was not around.

Speedy was really happy in his new home when, one day, four other dogs came running up and chased him around the yard. He barely made it back to safety. He would have to watch out for them in the future!

One day, the big dog was in the yard looking for something. "Have you seen my bone, Rabbit? I know I left it here. Oh, there it is, under the barn. I can't reach it." He tried to get it with his paw and his mouth, but he was too big.

Speedy tried to help. He pushed on the bone and was finally able to kick it out to where the dog could reach it. "Thanks, Rabbit," said the big, black dog. "Someday, maybe I can do you a favor."

A few days later, Speedy was careless. He was in the garden eating juicy carrot tops when the pack of dogs came back. He was surrounded by angry dogs with no place to run. "I've had it this time," Speedy thought to himself. "There's no way out."

Just then he heard a huge, deep bark. It was the big, black dog. He came up to the other dogs and let out a growl that showed he meant business. The other dogs took off and never even looked back. Speedy looked at the big dog and let out a big sigh. He hopped up to the big dog, rubbed against him, and said, "Thanks, Big Dog."

GO >

7 **What did Speedy find out through this experience?**

A Never trust a dog.

B Do not eat carrots from a vegetable garden.

C Doing good deeds can pay off in the future.

D There's no place like home.

8 **This story is *mostly* about a rabbit who —**

F found a home and a friend.

G did something foolish.

H had only bad things happen to him.

J was chased out of the vegetable garden.

9 **Why did Speedy come to live under the barn?**

A He was tired of his old home.

B Dogs chased him away from his old home in the field.

C He had to leave home because he was grown.

D His old home had been destroyed.

10 **What words in the story show that Speedy felt safe in his new home?**

F He even drank water from the big dog's dish...

G Speedy tried to help.

H Green plants were lined up in rows...

J The next day he let the dog see him...

11 **This story is most like a —**

A true story.

B fairy tale.

C mystery.

D folktale.

12 **When Speedy first met Big Dog, he probably felt —**

F comfortable.

G angry.

H frightened.

J foolish.

13 **What will probably happen next?**

A Speedy will find his family and go away with them.

B Big Dog and Speedy will become good friends.

C The pack of dogs won't come back to the garden.

D Big Dog and Speedy will have other adventures.

GO

Joseph and the Cactus

Joseph and his family were on vacation in Mexico. They had visited the markets, explored ancient ruins, and had gone fishing. It was an exciting and fun vacation.

One day, they drove out into the desert. They went in the early morning and made sure they took a shade tent with them, as well as plenty of water. Joseph had read about cactus at school for a report and wanted to see as many as he could. He knew that there are over 2,000 kinds of cactus. More kinds of cactus grow in Mexico than anywhere else. He wanted to dig one up and take it home with him.

Even early in the day, it was growing hot as Joseph and his family admired the beautiful cactus flowers. "They don't look like any other flowers I've ever seen," said his mother. His younger sister added, "Red, yellow, orange, purple, white, brown, pink. Look at all the different colors."

Joseph remembered his report and explained that, "Most cactus blossoms do not last long. Did you know that cactus have fruit, also? Some people say all cactus fruit can be eaten. The birds like the fruit and even the flesh of the plant. Did you know that if a person was without water in the desert he could break open a piece of cactus and get the water stored inside?"

"Ouch! You would have to get past those awful stickers first," laughed his sister.

"Ranchers sometimes burn the spines off and feed the cactus to their cattle when it is really dry and there is no grass for them," Joseph told his family. "The cattle seem to enjoy it."

"I'm glad you studied about cactus," his father said, "but I think we had better have a cool drink and then head back to town. Did you find a cactus to take home, Son?"

"No, they are so beautiful here in their natural home, I'm just going to take some pictures. I'm not sure that the people would let me carry it across the border anyway. The spines would be a problem. I'd rather remember the cactus the way they are here, with the sand, the blossoms, and the mountains in the distance," he answered.

GO

14 **What purpose do the spines on cactus serve?**

   F Attracting bees to the plant

   G Saving water for the plant

   H Protecting the plant from animals

   J Making the plant beautiful

15 **What will probably happen next?**

   A The family will continue their vacation trip.

   B Joseph will change his mind and dig up the cactus.

   C A big rainstorm will come.

   D The family will walk back to their hotel at the beach.

16 **The boxes show some things that happened in the story.**

Joseph and his family drove into the desert.		His sister found out about the stickers.
1	2	3

Which of these belongs in Box 2?

   F Joseph read about cactus for a school project.

   G Joseph told the family about cactus.

   H Joseph decided not to dig up a cactus and bring it home.

   J The family headed back to the hotel.

17 **Why did Joseph decide not to dig up a cactus to take home?**

   A It was too hot to dig out in the sun then.

   B His sister begged him not to do it.

   C It was against the law to dig up cactus.

   D He decided it belonged in the desert.

18 **Which of these would *most* help a reader understand the story?**

   F Looking up the word "cactus" in a dictionary

   G Going to the desert or botanical garden to see cactus in bloom

   H Watching television programs about the desert

   J Talking with friends who have been to the desert

19 **Which word best describes Joseph's day?**

   A Confusing

   B Exhausting

   C Enjoyable

   D Dangerous

Prickly Pear Cactus

Fruit
Spines
Paddle

Is this a picnic?

On Friday afternoon, Marta hurried home from school. The other children were planning picnics, trips, or other things for the weekend. Their plans sounded wonderful, and Marta wished she could do similar things. Marta did not look forward to the weekend. She and her family worked very hard all weekend. Marta was glad for Monday morning to come so she could go back to school.

Marta's family worked picking fruit and vegetables for farmers in the valley near their home. At winter harvest time, there was always more work to be done than there were workers. Marta's father explained that everyone had to help so that the family could buy the things they needed.

On Saturday, Marta's job was to watch the baby and to help pick fruit on low branches. The sun would be hot before the day was over. Marta had to move the baby to be sure he was in the shade. She had to give him his bottle. She was sure every girl in her fourth grade class had more wonderful things to do today than watch a baby and pick oranges.

The family came back to the truck at lunchtime. Marta's mother spread out the picnic on a cloth. The family ate the delicious food that she had made. The grown-ups lay down on the blankets in the shade and rested and played with the baby. Marta's brothers tossed a baseball for a while and then sat with them. Marta's mother and father told stories about life long ago. Marta loved hearing the stories. After a while, everyone ate some of the sweet, delicious oranges just off the trees. Then they returned to their harvest.

When they finished on Sunday evening, Marta smiled and remembered the stories and the food. It was fun to have the whole family together, and the work wasn't really that hard. Her father had said they would earn hundreds of dollars for their work. The family would be able to go shopping later for new clothes and things for the house. That would be a good time for everyone. "We really did go out to the country and have a family picnic," Marta thought. "We just did things that other people don't do. Besides, we got paid for our picnic."

GO

20 How did Marta's feelings change from the beginning of the story to the end?

    F She was happy at first and happier later.

    G She was unhappy at first and happy later.

    H She was happy at first and disappointed later.

    J She was unhappy at first and angry later.

21 Which of these probably happened after the story ended?

    A Marta became a farmer when she grew up.

    B The family went to a mall.

    C Her brothers quit school to go to work.

    D Marta told her friends at school a story about her weekend.

22 What lesson does this story teach?

    F The best way to have fun is to work with your family.

    G A fourth grader is too young to watch a baby.

    H Families can have fun together, even when they are working.

    J Parents should not make their children work.

23 What time of year did the story take place?

    A Spring

    B Summer

    C Fall

    D Winter

24 In the story, Marta did all of these *except* —

    F prepare lunch.

    G watch the baby.

    H pick oranges.

    J have a picnic.

25 At lunchtime, which of these happened?

    A Marta's father played the guitar and sang.

    B Marta's mother took a nap under an orange tree.

    C Marta's brothers played ball.

    D Marta read a book.

GO

For numbers 26 through 29, choose the best answer to the question.

26 Which of these sentences about a new breakfast cereal is <u>not</u> an opinion?

F Snappies taste better than the cereal you eat now.

G A box of Snappies contains 16 ounces of cereal.

H Snappies will help you stay happy the whole day.

J People who eat Snappies enjoy themselves better than those who don't.

27 Raquel is reading a story called "The Mystery of the House on the Hill."

Which of these sentences is probably the last one in the story?

A Everyone in town was certain the old Sanford house was haunted.

B With the mystery solved, Clyde left the house with his friends and headed back down the hill.

C They quietly walked up the steps and looked in the window.

D The basement door was open slightly, and they were sure that the noise they heard was coming from behind the door.

28 Which of these sentences states an opinion?

F There are fifty states in the United States.

G The largest state is Alaska, and the smallest is Delaware.

H The people in Kansas work harder than those in Nebraska.

J The Colorado River provides water to the people in many western states.

29 Which of these statements describes the setting for a story?

A A stream flowed through the desert canyon, providing the moisture needed for plants and animals to thrive.

B Coyotes often travel in packs and sometimes begin to howl for no apparent reason.

C When the Steen family left St. Louis, they had no idea how difficult their trip to California would be.

D Everyone was overjoyed when they discovered the stream flowing out of the desert canyon.

E1

Ever since he was a child, Roberto wanted to play professional baseball. He practiced almost every day, played whenever he could, and read about all the great players. While he was in high school, Roberto achieved his dream and was chosen by a professional team. To everyone's surprise, he turned the offer down. He wanted to attend college first before he made baseball his career.

A **What do you think will most likely happen after Roberto finishes college?**

A He will play another professional sport.

B He will write books about baseball.

C He will play professional baseball.

D He will coach basketball.

Here is a passage about an activity that many Americans enjoy. Read the passage and then do numbers 1 through 7 on page 141.

Nothing symbolizes summer in America more than cooking over a grill. In almost every American home, summer holidays are celebrated with a "cookout" in the backyard, on the deck, or anywhere a grill can be set up. The smell of sizzling food on a warm breeze is one of the memories of summer all of us remember fondly on cold winter days.

The word "barbecue" is sometimes used to describe food that is cooked on a grill. Its use can be confusing, however, because "barbecue" has several other meanings. Meat cooked over or in an open pit of coals is considered barbecue, as is meat that is slowly roasted in an oven or simmered in a sauce. Whatever you call it—grilled or barbecued—food cooked over an open flame has a special flavor that normal food lacks.

Traditional cookout fare is the hot dog and hamburger. Steaks are served on special occasions, and for people trying to cut the fat out of their diet, chicken and fish can be cooked on the grill.

Many people are surprised to learn that vegetables can be prepared deliciously on a grill. Potatoes develop an exciting new flavor when cooked on a grill, as do corn, peppers, and onions. Tomatoes, mushrooms, and squash can also be grilled, but they take a little more effort than firmer vegetables. These soft vegetables can be easily overcooked, and they will fall through the spaces in the grill.

The simplest grilling is done over charcoal that has been burned until it is red-hot. For added taste, wood chips from oak, mesquite, or other trees can be added to the charcoal. The most convenient grills burn a gas, like propane, that heats special rocks made from volcanic lava. Gas grills are among the most popular because they are so simple to use and heat quickly to cooking temperature.

GO

1   According to this passage, which of these is a soft vegetable?

   A   Tomatoes

   B   Potatoes

   C   Peppers

   D   Onions

2   Which of these is the best title for the passage?

   F   "Delicious Foods"

   G   "Four Ways to Cook Food"

   H   "The Great American Cookout"

   J   "Meats and Vegetables"

3   According to the passage, which of these foods is lowest in fat?

   A   Hot dogs

   B   Steaks

   C   Chicken

   D   Hamburgers

4   Which of these is <u>not</u> an advantage of cooking on a gas grill?

   F   Convenience

   G   Quick heating

   H   Traditional barbecue flavor

   J   Wood flavor

5   What does the word "fare" mean in the phrase "traditional cookout fare"?

   A   Open pit cooking

   B   Food

   C   Flavor

   D   Mesquite grilling

6   This passage suggests that—

   F   food cooked over a grill is better for you than food cooked in an oven.

   G   it is difficult to cook vegetables on a barbecue grill.

   H   cooking over a grill is something many Americans enjoy.

   J   slow roasting is the best way to prepare meat and vegetables.

7   Many people are _____ that some vegetables can be cooked on a grill.

   Which of these words indicates that many people don't know about cooking vegetables on a grill.

   A   unaware

   B   satisfied

   C   confident

   D   relieved

GO >

Read the passage and questions. Choose the answer that is better than the others.

In New York Harbor stands one of the most recognized figures in the world, the Statue of Liberty. This 150-foot tall statue, a gift from the people of France to the American people, honored the 1876 Centennial celebration, America's one hundredth birthday.

The statue, a creation of Frederic Auguste Bartholdi, was first assembled in Paris in 1884. It has a wrought-iron framework designed by Gustave Eiffel, who also designed the Eiffel Tower in Paris. After being assembled, it was disassembled and shipped across the Atlantic Ocean. The Statue of Liberty was then completely reassembled on a base planned by Richard Morris Hunt, a noted American architect.

The Statue of Liberty and its base were paid for in an unusual way, without government help. Instead, the people of France made contributions for the statue, and the people of America made contributions for the base. Among the contributors were many school children, who took great pride in knowing that their pennies helped to build such a wonderful monument.

Even though the outside of the Statue of Liberty is made of copper, it does not appear copper colored. Exposure to the air over the years has turned the skin a bluish-green color, which is known as verdigris.

On October 26, 1886, the Statue of Liberty was unveiled in its permanent location in New York Harbor. On its base was a plaque with a poem written by Emma Lazarus welcoming immigrants to the new land. Two lines near the end of the poem summarizes the statue's spirit: "Give me your tired, your poor, your huddled masses yearning to breathe free." Thousands of people were at the unveiling, and since then, millions have visited this symbol of freedom.

8 **What makes the Statue of Liberty different from many other monuments?**

F It celebrated freedom.

G It was paid for by the people of two countries, not the government.

H It was much taller than any other monument.

J It was made by a French sculptor.

9 **Based on what you read in the passage, when was the United States "born?"**

A 1776

B 1876

C 1884

D 1886

10 **Why did school children feel proud of the Statue of Liberty?**

F They contributed money to help build the statue.

G They contributed money to help ship the statue to the United States.

H They had a contest to pick the poem for the base.

J They contributed money to help build the base.

11 **Who planned the base on which the Statue of Liberty stands?**

A Gustave Eiffel

B Richard Hunt

C Frederic Bartholdi

D Emma Lazarus

12 **Why did the Statue of Liberty have to be disassembled so it could be shipped to America?**

F It was too large for any ship at the time to carry it.

G The copper skin was beginning to turn green.

H It was a gift to the American people for the Centennial.

J The people of Paris wanted to see it first.

13 **Why do you think the poem by Emma Lazarus was chosen for the plaque on the Statue of Liberty?**

A Emma Lazarus was a famous American poet.

B The poem and the statue both welcomed immigrants.

C It refers to the people of France who gave the statue to America.

D No one else wanted to write a poem about the statue.

GO

The Hardest Thing Ever

"This is a big commitment, kids. You'll have to help take care of the puppy and train her. Most of all, you'll have to be willing to give her up in a year."

When Mom said that, I really didn't think very much about it. I was too excited to be getting our first puppy. But today I really understand what she meant. Giving up Rachel was the hardest thing ever.

The day we picked Rachel up was one of the best in my life. My sister, Tina, and I raced from the car into the kennel. Mrs. Harbison was waiting for us, and on a leash beside her was the cutest, blackest, Labrador retriever I'd ever seen. We knelt down beside her and she licked our faces, nibbled our ears, and rolled over on her back between us. It was love at first sight for all of us.

On the way home from the kennel, Dad reminded us what we were doing. "Rachel isn't our dog forever, kids. We can keep her for only one year. Our job is to help Rachel get used to people and to give her basic training. A year from now, we have to return her to Mrs. Harbison so she can begin Rachel's real training as a guide dog. Someday, Rachel will become the guide and companion for a blind person. Rachel will do one of the most important jobs in the world."

To be honest, I heard every word Dad said and tried to believe him. I guess my head was thinking about what he said, but my heart didn't understand a word of it.

Every day, Rachel became more a part of our lives. She whined goodbye when we left for school in the morning and was waiting at the door when we returned. She slept in my room, but every once in a while wandered into Tina's room, just to check up on her. Rachel loved Mom and Dad, too, but it was clear she was my dog.

"Don't forget, Eddie, Rachel is only ours for a year. You can love her as much as you want, but we have to give her up next year." Mom and Dad must have said this a thousand times, and every time I nodded my head. My heart, however, still didn't believe it.

The months went by, and Rachel grew into a big dog. She went swimming with me, chased sticks and balls, and learned how much fun the snow could be. Our cat, Patches, even fell in love with Rachel. Whenever Rachel curled up for a nap, Patches would run right over and snuggle up between her legs.

It was a rainy day in November when we had to bring Rachel back to Mrs. Harbison. I thought I was going to die. On the way to the kennel, Rachel sat between Tina and me as if she knew what was happening. When we arrived at the kennel, I wasn't sure I could even get out of the car.

Then something happened that made me feel a little better. Mrs. Harbison walked over to the car with a young woman holding her arm. We could see that she was blind.

"This is Lauren Wolf. She and Rachel will be trained together. When they have finished their training, Rachel will be Lauren's dog."

GO

I never got over losing Rachel, not until last week. We received an invitation to Rachel's graduation from guide dog school. At first, I didn't want to go, but my folks talked me into it. I'm glad they did. When I saw Rachel and Lauren, I knew we had done the right thing. Rachel remembered me, but it was clear she was Lauren's dog now. I could also see that Lauren had a better life because of Rachel. A year ago, Lauren often needed help getting around. Today, she moved around confidently and capably. Through Rachel, we had helped Lauren become a fully independent person.

On the way home, I said something I thought I never would. I asked Mom and Dad if we could get another guide dog.

14 Who is telling this story?

   F Mom   **H** Tina

   G Dad   **J** Eddie

15 What was the "hardest thing"?

   A giving up Rachel   **C** meeting Lauren Wolf

   B training Rachel   **D** going to Rachel's graduation

16 In this story, Eddie learns that —

   F it is important to listen to parents, even if you don't like what they say.

   G doing the right thing can often be difficult.

   H raising a puppy is harder work than it looks.

   J dogs usually like one person in a family more than the others.

17 Which of these describes how Eddie's feelings changed during the story?

   A He was happy for a year, then was sad, and never became happy again.

   B He was happy for a year, then was angry when he had to give up Rachel.

   C He was happy for a year, then was sad, and eventually became happy again.

   D At first he was happy, but became sad and never wanted a dog again.

GO

STRAWBERRIES

Almost everyone likes strawberries. They are sweet, juicy, and good for you, too. They contain more vitamin C than oranges or grapefruit, and are high in fiber. Strawberries grow in the wild where they have very sweet fruit. Birds love them, but they are so small people don't often eat them. Strawberries from a home garden are much bigger. They grow on a small vine that bears fruit after it is at least two years old.

Because they spoil easily, strawberries must be kept cool. They used to be a rare treat, but they are widely available in stores year-round now because refrigerated planes, trains, and trucks can carry them from farms around the country or the world to your local market.

People who need to be careful about eating too much sugar can enjoy strawberries. A whole cup of strawberries has about the same number of calories and natural fruit sugar as a half cup of many other fruits.

If you want to cut down on the amount of sugar you eat and still enjoy a sweet treat, here is a delicious, sugarless, strawberry jam you can make for the family.

You will need:
- 2 cups strawberries, washed, sliced, with green caps removed (or use frozen ones, without sugar)
- 1/4 cup frozen pineapple juice concentrate, thawed
- 1 cup mashed banana (mash ripe banana with a fork)
- 3 tablespoons cornstarch
- 3 tablespoons cold water

Mix strawberries, with their juice, and pineapple juice concentrate. Microwave on high for one minute. Stir mashed banana until it is creamy. Mix into strawberries and juice.

Combine cornstarch and water in a small bowl. Add to strawberries. Stir well. Microwave on high for 30 seconds. Stir. Microwave on high for 30 seconds. Stir. Continue until the jam is thick and is dark red. Cool. Store in refrigerator.

For family members who are not watching their sugar or calories, this jam would be good over ice cream or pound cake.

GO >

18 **Which of these is a fact stated in the article?**

F Wild strawberries are very sweet.

G The sugarless strawberry jam is delicious.

H Almost everyone likes strawberries.

J Strawberries grow on a small vine.

19 **How old must strawberry plants be before they bear fruit?**

A Three years

B Six months

C Two years

D One year

20 **Strawberries contain—**

F many vitamins and fewer calories than other fruit.

G many calories and fewer vitamins than other fruit.

H few calories and few vitamins.

J many calories and many vitamins.

21 **People can enjoy strawberries more now than they could years ago because —**

A there are more strawberry farms now than earlier.

B refrigerated transportation gets the berries to market more quickly.

C new varieties of strawberries have been developed.

D now people know more about how to make jam and other dishes.

22 **When you are making the jam, you must put it in the microwave and cook it, stir it, and then —**

F repeat the cooking and stirring until it is thick and dark.

G freeze the jam.

H stir it while the jam is cooking in the microwave.

J add sugar until it tastes good.

23 **The information in this article was written in order to —**

A explain how to grow strawberries.

B get the reader to eat healthful fruits and vegetables.

C tell about strawberries and provide a tasty recipe.

D get the reader to eat foods that have fewer calories.

GO

For numbers 24 through 27, choose the best answer to the question.

24   Robert lived with his father in a trailer near the river. The two of them spent every spare minute fishing or boating in the river. That's how they met Mrs. Herera, an energetic woman of 92 years who shared their love of the river.

What part of a story does this passage tell about?

F   The plot

G   The characters

H   The mood

J   The setting

25   **Which of these sentences states an opinion?**

A   The Comet is the most comfortable automobile you can buy.

B   The Comet is the longest car in its price range.

C   The price of the Comet is only $17,000.

D   The Comet averages 22 miles per gallon of gasoline in city driving.

26   Josephina is reading a book called *City Under the Ocean*.

Which of these sentences is probably the last one in the story?

F   The dome was finished, but now came the hard part, pumping the water out of the dome.

G   The world said they couldn't do it, but they did, and the residents of Sea City celebrated their first anniversary with a huge party.

H   "I have a suggestion you may find unbelievable," said Dr. Harrison, "but I have evidence it will work."

J   While the dome was being built, the government was looking for families who would be willing to give up their current lives and settle the new city.

27   **Which of these sentences about weight lifting is not an opinion?**

A   People who lift weights feel better than those who do not.

B   The more weight you lift, the better you look.

C   It is harder to lift weights than to swim or ski.

D   Weight lifting burns up fewer calories than running the same amount of time.

STOP

Spectrum Vocabulary Grade 4

Grade 4 Answer Key

Page 106
- **A.** C
- **B.** H
- **1.** B
- **2.** J
- **3.** C
- **4.** F
- **5.** D
- **6.** G
- **7.** A
- **8.** G

Page 107
- **A.** D
- **B.** H
- **1.** A
- **2.** G
- **3.** D
- **4.** H
- **5.** C
- **6.** G
- **7.** A

Page 108
- **A.** A
- **B.** J
- **1.** C
- **2.** H
- **3.** D
- **4.** F
- **5.** C
- **6.** G
- **7.** A
- **8.** J

Page 109
- **A.** A
- **B.** G
- **1.** B
- **2.** J
- **3.** A
- **4.** J
- **5.** A

Page 110
- **A.** B
- **B.** F
- **1.** A
- **2.** J
- **3.** B
- **4.** G
- **5.** C
- **6.** F

Page 111
- **A.** C
- **B.** F
- **1.** C
- **2.** F
- **3.** B
- **4.** J
- **5.** D
- **6.** H

Page 112
- **E1.** D
- **E2.** H
- **1.** C
- **2.** J
- **3.** C
- **4.** G
- **5.** A
- **6.** H
- **7.** D
- **8.** G

Page 113
- **9.** C
- **10.** G
- **11.** B
- **12.** H
- **13.** D
- **14.** F
- **15.** B
- **16.** F
- **17.** B
- **18.** J
- **19.** C

Page 114
- **20.** F
- **21.** C
- **22.** J
- **23.** C
- **24.** H
- **25.** C
- **26.** J
- **27.** C

Page 115
- **28.** H
- **29.** B
- **30.** J
- **31.** B
- **32.** F
- **33.** D
- **34.** H
- **35.** B

Page 116
- **E1.** D
- **E2.** F
- **1.** B
- **2.** F
- **3.** A
- **4.** J
- **5.** B
- **6.** H
- **7.** D
- **8.** F

Page 117
- **9.** A
- **10.** J
- **11.** C
- **12.** G
- **13.** A
- **14.** J
- **15.** C
- **16.** G
- **17.** B
- **18.** F
- **19.** D

Grade 4 Answer Key

Page 118
20. G
21. D
22. G
23. C
24. J
25. A
26. F
27. C

Page 119
28. H
29. D
30. F
31. D
32. H
33. B
34. J
35. A

Page 120
A. B
1. D
2. F
3. C
4. J

Page 121
A. B

Page 122
1. D
2. G
3. D
4. H
5. B
6. F
7. C

Page 124
8. F
9. B
10. J
11. A
12. G
13. C

Page 125
A. B

Page 126
1. B
2. F
3. A
4. H
5. B
6. J

Page 128
7. A
8. F
9. D
10. H
11. B
12. G
13. C

Page 130
14. J
15. C
16. G
17. A
18. G
19. D
20. H

Page 131
A. C

Page 132
1. D
2. H
3. C
4. F
5. B
6. F

Page 134
7. C
8. F
9. D
10. F
11. D
12. H
13. B

Page 136
14. H
15. A
16. G
17. D
18. G
19. C

Page 138
20. G
21. D
22. H
23. C
24 F
25. C

Page 139
26. G
27. B
28. H
29. A

Page 140
A. C

Grade 4 Answer Key

Page 141
1. A
2. H
3. C
4. J
5. B
6. H
7. A

Page 143
8. G
9. A
10. J
11. B
12. F
13. B

Page 145
14. J
15. A
16. G
17. C

Page 147
18. J
19. C
20. F
21. B
22. F
23. C

Page 148
24. J
25. A
26. G
27. D

Fill in only one letter for each item. If you change an answer, make sure to erase your first mark completely.

Page 106

A. (A) (B) (C) (D)

B. (F) (G) (H) (J)

1. (A) (B) (C) (D)

2. (F) (G) (H) (J)

3. (A) (B) (C) (D)

4. (F) (G) (H) (J)

5. (A) (B) (C) (D)

6. (F) (G) (H) (J)

7. (A) (B) (C) (D)

8. (F) (G) (H) (J)

Page 107

A. (A) (B) (C) (D)

B. (F) (G) (H) (J)

1. (A) (B) (C) (D)

2. (F) (G) (H) (J)

3. (A) (B) (C) (D)

4. (F) (G) (H) (J)

5. (A) (B) (C) (D)

6. (F) (G) (H) (J)

7. (A) (B) (C) (D)

Page 108

A. (A) (B) (C) (D)

B. (F) (G) (H) (J)

1. (A) (B) (C) (D)

2. (F) (G) (H) (J)

3. (A) (B) (C) (D)

4. (F) (G) (H) (J)

5. (A) (B) (C) (D)

6. (F) (G) (H) (J)

Page 109

A. (A) (B) (C) (D)

B. (F) (G) (H) (J)

1. (A) (B) (C) (D)

2. (F) (G) (H) (J)

3. (A) (B) (C) (D)

4. (F) (G) (H) (J)

5. (A) (B) (C) (D)

Page 110

A. (A) (B) (C) (D)

B. (F) (G) (H) (J)

1. (A) (B) (C) (D)

2. (F) (G) (H) (J)

3. (A) (B) (C) (D)

4. (F) (G) (H) (J)

5. (A) (B) (C) (D)

6. (F) (G) (H) (J)

Page 111

A. (A) (B) (C) (D)

B (F) (G) (H) (J)

1. (A) (B) (C) (D)

2. (F) (G) (H) (J)

3. (A) (B) (C) (D)

4. (F) (G) (H) (J)

5. (A) (B) (C) (D)

6. (F) (G) (H) (J)

Page 112

E1. (A) (B) (C) (D)

E2. (F) (G) (H) (J)

1. (A) (B) (C) (D)

2. (F) (G) (H) (J)

3. (A) (B) (C) (D)

4. (F) (G) (H) (J)

5. (A) (B) (C) (D)

6. (F) (G) (H) (J)

7. (A) (B) (C) (D)

8. (F) (G) (H) (J)

Page 113

9. (A) (B) (C) (D)

10. (F) (G) (H) (J)

11. (A) (B) (C) (D)

12. (F) (G) (H) (J)

13. (A) (B) (C) (D)

14. (F) (G) (H) (J)

15. (A) (B) (C) (D)

16. (F) (G) (H) (J)

17. (A) (B) (C) (D)

18. (F) (G) (H) (J)

19. (A) (B) (C) (D)

Page 114

20. (F) (G) (H) (J)

21. (A) (B) (C) (D)

22. (F) (G) (H) (J)

23. (A) (B) (C) (D)

24. (F) (G) (H) (J)

25. (A) (B) (C) (D)

26. (F) (G) (H) (J)

27. (A) (B) (C) (D)

Page 115

28. (F) (G) (H) (J)

29. (A) (B) (C) (D)

30. (F) (G) (H) (J)

31. (A) (B) (C) (D)

32. (F) (G) (H) (J)

33. (A) (B) (C) (D)

34. (F) (G) (H) (J)

35. (A) (B) (C) (D)

Page 116

E1. (A) (B) (C) (D)

E2. (F) (G) (H) (J)

1. (A) (B) (C) (D)

2. (F) (G) (H) (J)

3. (A) (B) (C) (D)

4. (F) (G) (H) (J)

5. (A) (B) (C) (D)

6. (F) (G) (H) (J)

7. (A) (B) (C) (D)

8. (F) (G) (H) (J)

Page 117

9. (A) (B) (C) (D)

10. (F) (G) (H) (J)

11. (A) (B) (C) (D)

12. (F) (G) (H) (J)

13. (A) (B) (C) (D)

14. (F) (G) (H) (J)

15. (A) (B) (C) (D)

16. (F) (G) (H) (J)

17. (A) (B) (C) (D)

18. (F) (G) (H) (J)

19. (A) (B) (C) (D)

Page 118

20. (F) (G) (H) (J)

21. (A) (B) (C) (D)

22. (F) (G) (H) (J)

23. (A) (B) (C) (D)

24. (F) (G) (H) (J)

25. (A) (B) (C) (D)

Test-taking Student Answer Sheet

26. F G H J

27. A B C D

Page 119

28. F G H J

29. A B C D

30. F G H J

31. A B C D

32. F G H J

33. A B C D

34. F G H J

35. A B C D

Page 120

A. A B C D

1. A B C D

2. F G H J

3. A B C D

4. F G H J

Page 121

A. A B C D

Page 122

1. A B C D

2. F G H J

3. A B C D

4. F G H J

5. A B C D

6. F G H J

7. A B C D

Page 124

8. F G H J

9. A B C D

10. F G H J

11. A B C D

12. F G H J

13. A B C D

Page 125

A. A B C D

Page 126

1. A B C D

2. F G H J

3. A B C D

4. F G H J

5. A B C D

6. F G H J

Page 128

7. A B C D

8. F G H J

9. A B C D

10. F G H J

11. A B C D

12. F G H J

13. A B C D

Page 130

14. F G H J

15. A B C D

16. F G H J

17. A B C D

18. F G H J

19. A B C D

20. F G H J

Page 131

A. A B C D

Page 132

1. A B C D

2. F G H J

3. A B C D

4. F G H J

5. A B C D

6. F G H J

Page 134

7. A B C D

8. F G H J

9. A B C D

10. F G H J

11. A B C D

12. F G H J

13. A B C D

Page 136

14. F G H J

15. A B C D

16. F G H J

17. A B C D

18. F G H J

19. A B C D

Page 138

20. F G H J

21. A B C D

22. F G H J

23. A B C D

24. F G H J

25. A B C D

Page 139

26. F G H J

27. A B C D

28. F G H J

29. A B C D

Page 140

A. A B C D

Page 141

1. A B C D

2. F G H J

3. A B C D

4. F G H J

5. A B C D

6. F G H J

7. A B C D

Page 143

8. F G H J

9. A B C D

10. F G H J

11. A B C D

12. F G H J

13. A B C D

Page 145

14. F G H J

15. A B C D

16. F G H J

17. A B C D

Page 147

18. F G H J

19. A B C D

20. F G H J

21. A B C D

22. F G H J

23. A B C D

Page 148

24. F G H J

25. A B C D

26. F G H J

27. A B C D

Notes

Notes

Notes